**BESTSELLING BOOKS BY KRISTEN MARTIN**

**NONFICTION**

*Be Your Own #Goals*

**FICTION**

*Shadow Crown*

*Renegade Cruex*

*The Alpha Drive*

*The Order of Omega*

*Restitution*

*To Marisa: What is meant for you will always find you*

DISCOVER YOUR SOUL PURPOSE, WORK YOUR
LIGHT, AND LIVE THE LIFE YOU DESERVE

Soul FLOW

FROM AMAZON BESTSELLING AUTHOR

KRISTEN MARTIN

Black Falcon Press

Black Falcon Press, LLC

P.O. Box 1879

Montgomery, TX 77356

http://www.blackfalconpress.com

Library of Congress Control Number: 2019905028

ISBN: 978-0-9979092-7-2 (paperback)

First paperback edition: August 2019

10 9 8 7 6 5 4 3 2 1

*For those who seek their truth --*
*may you find it here.*

# contents

soul FLOW

# introduction

I THOUGHT WRITING a second personal development book would be easier than the first, but boy, was I in for a rude awakening. I've been on what I like to call a *spiritual journey* for a few years now, and every time I sit down to write, I think, "Okay, I'm ready to write this book. I've got this all figured out." But then, when I actually *do* sit down to write, I realize I absolutely do *not* have it all figured out. My head gets in the way more often than not, and some days are chock full of creativity; others make me want to hole up in my room and never show my face again.

But I always come back to it. Writing, that is. It's one of the only things that makes sense to me, even when it doesn't. How's that for irony? If you're a writer, I'm sure you understand. And if not, one day . . . you will.

I digress. Back to my spiritual journey.

My wake-up call came in the form of precancerous cells in the year of 2015. That was also the year I decided to finally pursue my lifelong dream of becoming an author and self-published my first work of fiction, *The Alpha Drive*. Normally I would go into the backstory, but I already did that in my first personal development book, *Be Your Own #Goals*. Recounting that experience always leaves me feeling grateful and at the same time overwhelmed with grief, because I know just how quickly life can be snatched away from us. But if there's one thing that experience taught me, it's that we cannot live in fear—and I stopped living in fear when I woke up in that hospital bed in October of 2015.

I came to a startling realization recently, and it's what sparked the inspiration for this book. After diving into more self-help books than I care to admit (believe me, it was a lot), I felt my mind opening up in ways that it never had before. Through traveling, reading, journaling, and meditation, these shifts in perspective have truly awakened my soul. And it hasn't been *just* an awakening, but a full-blown transformation.

A soulful foray into my subconscious.

That's where our true self lives. In our subconscious.

It's also where our *soulflow* lives.

Now, I know "soulflow" isn't a word. In fact, it kind of sounds like the word *soulful*. While they may sound similar, soulflow means something completely different. Sure, it's a word I made up—but it perfectly and so wholly encompasses the message I want to share with you throughout this book. I resonated with this new word of mine so much that I decided to use it as the title. Perhaps it resonates with you, too—and that's why you're here in this very moment, reading this introduction.

Soulflow is about so much more than reading self-help books, journaling, meditating, and striving to live your best life. It's about true self-awareness and why we behave the way we do. Why we want the things we want. Why we think the things we think. Getting to the root of all this will not only help you . . . it will forever change you—and in ways you cannot even begin to fathom.

So if you've been feeling lost, stuck, trapped, hopeless, numb, uninspired, or disengaged, I sincerely hope that this book will help you see past whatever it is you're going through. I hope it'll help you cultivate a sense of inner peace and calm. I hope it'll encourage you to discover and/or renew your soul purpose and live to that standard every single day. I hope that in sharing my journey and experiences, you'll be able to tap into your soulflow, too.

# How to use this Book:

This book is meant to be well-loved and well-used. At the end of each chapter, you will find a space for self-reflection. I know it may be tempting to breeze through this book in one sitting (as I tend to do whenever I get my hands on a new personal development book), but in order to truly absorb the information being presented to you, it's imperative to complete the self-reflection immediately after reading each chapter. I can share my experiences and my journey with you until the cows come home (and I most certainly do throughout this book), but until you actually put these principles into practice, do a little soul traversing, and reflect on your thoughts, feelings, behaviors, and actions . . . they're just words on a page. Some of these reflections may be harder than others and that's okay. If anything, that's just your *soulflow* trying to find you. Instead of pushing her away . . . let her in.

# chapter one

## THE BALI SOUL AWAKENING

IN SEPTEMBER OF 2018, I had the incredible opportunity to teach at a writing retreat in Bali, Indonesia. It was there, in a stunning villa surrounded by eleven other amazing women, that I experienced my first true soul awakening.

While the health scare I had experienced just a few years prior to this trip was certainly a wake-up call, I wouldn't exactly call it a *soul awakening*. It was more of a slap in the face—a startling realization that, even though I'd followed all of society's rules and followed its mind-numbing path to "success", my life wasn't what I'd hoped it would be.

That particular wake-up call was like stepping into the ocean in the middle of winter, bouncing back and forth between your feet because it's so damn frigid. My soul awakening in Bali was much less in-your-face; I'd compare it to a flower blooming at the beginning of spring—slow, gentle, delicate . . . a natural progression after winter has passed.

I spent two magical weeks in Bali—and when I say magical, I'm not over-exaggerating. I've never felt more connected, more aligned, more *at peace* than when I was there. The simplistic lifestyle of the locals was truly something to behold. In western society, where we're taught to strive for *more*—do *more*, be *more*, achieve *more*—well, I witnessed the exact opposite mindset in Bali.

*Being* was more important than *doing*.

I remember, clear as day, waking up in the morning in a room that had just a bed, an overhead fan, and a nightstand. No alarm clock. No television. No PlayStation or Xbox. No stereo. No distractions.

Each morning when I awoke, my eyes fixated on the slow, steady whirring of the bamboo fan blades overhead. My gaze would follow the ceiling as it converged into a pyramid-like shape—as if I were lying on my back on the inside of said pyramid, staring upward at the pointed top. Instead of reaching for my phone to check social media and emails, I'd stare at the fan and just breathe. I'd slowly stretch my body, starting with pointing my toes, then bending my knees, then wiggling my fingers, until I was sitting upright, rolling my neck from side to side. I'd take my time getting out of bed, putting my glasses on before sliding the double doors open to the terrace that awaited just outside my bedroom.

Immediately, I was greeted with the sound of chirping birds, buzzing insects, rustling leaves, and the steady flow of water. Barefoot, I walked along the stone path, noticing the beautiful array of flowers, plants, and foliage lining the villa. A couple of small Buddha statues sat at the far end of the pathway, and as I made my way over to them, I couldn't help but notice the smooth texture beneath my feet. Each step I took brought a renewed sense of energy, mindfulness, and connection.

As I sat in front of one of the statues, I noticed the lines that made up each angle and contour—the cracks and wear from its many days in the sun—and the beautiful vines growing up the wall behind it. When a bee buzzed near my ear and zoomed right across my face, I didn't so much as flinch. I didn't freak out or try to swat it away or get up and move to a place where the bee wasn't . . .

*Because the bee is everywhere* (more on this in a minute).

Instead, I sat there with my eyes closed, allowing thoughts to come and go like leaves in the autumn breeze. I sat and sat and sat. I just *was*.

It was the first moment I experienced just *being*.

No agenda. No intentions. No action. Just being.

When was the last time you allowed yourself to just be? Do you even know how to experience this state? Think back to this morning. Are you able to describe, in detail, how it played out for you? Are you able to tell me the sounds your ears brought to life? The feelings that washed over you as you walked into your kitchen to make your morning cup of coffee? What your eyes had the privilege of seeing at each interval of time?

Or was this morning a flurry of chaos as you rushed to the next thing, the next action item, the next destination, the next whatever-isn't-this-present-moment?

Future, future, future. We always seem to be looking forward, and because of this, we tend to miss what's right in front of us—what's staring us directly in the face, begging for us to take notice and *appreciate* everything it is. Because when you really think about it, this moment, right here—you absorbing the words in this book—is all you truly have. Are you fully present? Are you taking it all in? Or is your mind trying to distract you? What about the dishes in the sink? The laundry sitting in the dryer? The twenty plus emails you have yet to answer?

Take a moment to look up from this book. Close your eyes. Count to three and simultaneously inhale deeply through your nose, then count to three again and exhale through your mouth. Repeat two more times. Then, open your eyes and take in your surroundings.

What do you see?

What do you hear?

How do you feel?

Be. All. Here.

Let's go back to the bee. *The bee is everywhere.* What do I mean by this? The bee, like so many other things in our lives, is an external stimulus. You and I both know that I couldn't control the trajectory of that bee, or the fact that it chose to cross my path while I was sitting in front of the Balinese statue. Instead of trying to escape from the bee, I embraced it and waited for it to pass. Because, in time, everything passes. *This too shall pass.*

When we try too hard to change the present moment or control the outcome, we're essentially trying to force our own hand—and our hand usually has no say in what's bound to happen anyway. Everything will naturally unfold exactly when and how it's supposed to.

Just like this soul awakening in Bali.

It's not something I could have forced. It's not something I could have controlled. And it's certainly not something I could have planned for. Honestly, it wouldn't have been nearly as impactful if it'd happened any other way, in any other place, at any other time.

How did I know I was experiencing a *true* soul awakening? The answer is quite simple, really. It was the first time I experienced *pure bliss.*

Sure, at different points in my life, I've experienced happiness, excitement, cloud nine, over-the-moon type feelings . . . but they were always fleeting. Achieving goals, buying nice things, and getting praise are all wonderful—but these feelings are fleeting because they are brought about by external forces.

Something *outside* of ourselves.

In Bali, for the first time in my life, I was sincerely happy to just be me. I didn't think about my personal belongings. I didn't think about how much money I did or didn't have in the bank. I didn't think about my outstanding goals or where I'd potentially fallen short. I didn't think about my weight or anything related to my body image . . .

Can you even imagine having a full day free of worry, anxiety, or forward-focused thoughts? Can you imagine having that for two weeks? What about for a lifetime?

Being immersed in Bali culture taught me that, more than anything, we, as humans, crave *connection*—not only with others, but also with *ourselves*. I remember walking down unpaved roads past the many tents, smiling and waving at the shop owners who weren't stressed or worried or focused on anything but what was right in front of them. There was such a sense of ease when it came to their demeanor—like deep down, they knew everything would be okay. Like they would always be taken care of, no matter what. No winter lasts forever; no spring skips its bloom.

That sense of *believing* in a life of ease and simplicity rubbed off on me in a big way. Things that would normally get me worked up just . . . didn't. I remember sitting in a Balinese restaurant, completely calm and patient even when my food was served what must have been an hour after it'd been ordered. I remember skinny-dipping in the private pool in my Seminyak villa in the middle of the night—just me, the stars, and the moon. I remember wanting to cradle and take care of the baby monkey that jumped onto my lap in the Monkey Forest. I remember approaching an elephant for the very first time and laying my palm against its trunk, tears springing to my eyes as an ethereal connection, unlike anything I've ever experienced, was made. In these moments, I felt alive. I felt whole. I felt connected to something so much bigger . . .

Because that's just it. Life is so much more than what your day-to-day looks like, what you do for a living, what your financial situation is, what your family circumstances are. Life is about BEING. Here and now. In this present moment. Experiencing. Feeling. Connecting.

We spend so much time outside of ourselves that rarely do we actually look inside—rarely do we get the *opportunity* to even do so. How messed up is that? We're so consumed by media, responsibilities, and pleasing everyone else except ourselves that we can't even take the time to get to know who we actually are at our core and to *sit* with that part of ourselves—to just *be* with all that we actually are.

Let me ask you something. At your core . . . what is your essence? What speaks to your soul? What do you value above all else? What do you hope to do with this one precious life you've been given?

Life is not meant to be stressful, busy, or chaotic. You were not made to run on little to no sleep, make poor choices that wreak havoc on your body and mind, say yes to things when you really want to say no, and work your life away so that you can wither away in a retirement home never having experienced life. YOUR life.

You were not made to live in fear of the unknown.

You were made to embrace it . . .

As the truest, most authentic version of yourself.

And if you don't know who that person is or what she even looks like—that's okay. That's exactly why I'm writing this book. For so many years, I did what everyone else expected of me. Never did I once think to set my own standards. To define my own expectations. To determine what happiness, success, fulfillment, and joy look like *to me*.

Society, parents, teachers, mentors . . . in our younger years, they behave as a guidance system. We learn good from bad and right from wrong at a very young age. And while this *is* a starting point, that's all it really is. What many of us *never* realize is that all of these things—our beliefs, our values, our standards—are predetermined and so engrained that we don't even think twice about them. We don't ask questions. It just is the way it is. So we go about our lives following this roadmap that isn't even ours to begin with . . . and we wonder why we're confused, unhappy, and out of touch with ourselves. It's because we never tapped into ourselves—into our *soulflow*—in the first place!

Of course, this is no fault of our own. When we're young, we absorb *everything*. From there, we piece together what we can and try to make some sense out of life. Many develop a "moral compass" and thereby try to do right by others. This is all well and good—again, as a starting point—but there must come a time when we dare to ask the tough questions. When we think, "Hmm, that doesn't sit right with me", and actually *do* something about it. When we muster up enough courage to bulldoze the roads on our map that don't align with who we truly are and begin to build new ones.

That's what my soul awakening did for me. It initiated the process of asking the questions I'd never thought to ask, acting on the things that made my stomach turn, and daring to change the roads that had been so strategically laid out before me.

*Find your other half—someone to "complete" you—and live a lifetime of happiness!* Sorry Disney, not buying it. New road, please.

*Be married and have kids by the time you're thirty or be destined for a lonely life with your eight cats!* Who says I can't like cats? Depends on your version of happiness, doesn't it? New road, please.

*Reduce your caloric intake and over-exercise to look like a Victoria's Secret Model!* Sorry, but I love myself too much to deny my taste buds of all the delicious wine, cheese, bread, and chocolate this world has to offer. New road, please.

*Work a corporate job, even if it makes you miserable, so that you'll be considered successful in society's eyes!* If success equals misery, why would I want any part of it? New road, please.

New road, new road, NEW ROAD.

You have the power to build new roads—but if your roadmap is already so congested cruising along the 405, the 101, and all the other interstates mentioned in the Billboard Top 100 songs from the 2000s . . . it might just be time to take a back-road. Just like you would when you're driving, dare to ask the same questions about life:

Is there another way?

Is there, perhaps, a *better* way?

Most likely, there is. Be brave enough to take it.

We don't know what we don't know. I'm about to share all of the things *I* didn't know until my Bali soul awakening transpired. My hope is that, at the very least, it'll inspire you to start asking questions.

It's time to get uncomfortable, my friends.

We've got a whole lotta nonsense to work through.

## Reflection

Spend some time considering what beliefs you've lived by your entire life. In the space below, list all of your beliefs around relationships, success, happiness, health, love, and anything else you can think of. If you can recall, write down where that belief came from (like your parents, grandparents, society, religious background, etc.). We'll refer back to this list in the next chapter's reflection.

_____

_____

_____

_____

_____

_____

_____

_____

_____

_____

_____

_____

_____

_____

_____

_____

_____

_____

_____

_____

_____

_____

_____

_____

_____

_____

# chapter two

## THE VICTIM MENTALITY

WE'RE STARTING OFF with a doozy because if you're guilty of playing the victim card in most (or all) situations, you may as well shut this book right now. I can't help you if you aren't willing to help yourself.

Period. End of story.

But, seeing as you picked up this book, it seems you *are* willing to help yourself. You *want* to tap into your soulflow, but haven't quite figured out how to, or what this even really means for you.

Those who constantly play the victim are often blind to the fact that this is what they're doing. It's a mental state that is so deep-seated, it's unrecognizable. I'm going to ask you a few questions and, without judging yourself, I want you to answer them.

Do you often find that you use phrases like . . .

"Can you believe that happened to me?"

"That's just my luck."

"That *would* happen to someone like me."

"I swear it feels like everyone's out to get me."

Are you judging yourself based on your answers? Don't! I'm sure we can all relate. I've used phrases like this a time or two (okay, maybe more). The problem with having—and nurturing—a victim mentality is that your thought process is grounded in negativity. It's focused on all the things that are going wrong instead of all the things that are going right, which snowballs into something even worse—the unwavering belief that things are going to be bad *no matter what*. You don't know exactly what's going to happen or how it's going to happen, but you *do* know that you're not going to like it.

Listen, if you're already telling yourself that you're never going to get promoted, or find a future partner, or start a family, or get out of debt . . . what chance do you really have? You've already *decided* you can't have it. And if you stay in that mindset, you never will.

Victim mentality is rooted in fear, specifically the fear of loss. Throughout this book, we'll talk about the many fears we, as humans, face because when it comes down to it, that's really the *only* thing standing in the way of experiencing your soulflow. Let me rephrase that, in case you didn't catch my drift. The *only* reason you haven't tapped into your soulflow is because *you are afraid of something*—loss, failure, rejection, inadequacy, not having enough, judgment, the unknown . . . you get the idea.

In case you've never heard of the Law of Attraction and Manifestation, allow me to be the first to give you a brief introduction. This *New Thought Movement* grew out of the teachings of Phineas Quimby in the early 19<sup>th</sup> century after he was diagnosed with tuberculosis and regained his health through his "mind over body" study. Over the years, these concepts have taken on many different forms (you may be familiar with the books *Think and Grow Rich* by Napoleon Hill and *The Secret* by Rhonda Byrne), but the underlying principle remains the same.

**Like attracts like.**

New Thought authors believe that the Law of Attraction is always working in the background of our lives, bringing to each person the conditions and experiences that they predominantly think about, whether good *or* bad. Which means if you're constantly playing the victim, always blaming others, and expecting the worst to happen . . . that's exactly what you'll attract—what you'll *manifest*—into your life.

Like attracts like.

Have you ever noticed that the more you think about something, the quicker it seems to suddenly appear in your reality? Like getting pulled over for speeding? Or your air conditioning unit breaking in the middle of summer? Or having the fire department unexpectedly show up at your house and kick down your front door? Or getting rear-ended for the first time when you've never been in a car accident? In case you're wondering, yes, I have had the pleasure of experiencing all of these things almost immediately after thinking about them—and I'm talking within a couple of days of the thought crossing my mind!

While all of these things might sound bad, something good came from each of them. The cop that pulled me over let me off with a warning—and had he not pulled me over, I probably wouldn't have slowed down in time for the family of deer crossing the street just a few blocks down the road. My A/C unit breaking was a pain, but it allowed me to spend quality time with a friend I hadn't seen in a while—at her place, of course, where the A/C was fully intact. I'd been thinking for *years* about getting a new front door, but hadn't wanted to drop the cash on one, so the fire department kicking it in beyond repair allowed me to do just that. And getting rear-ended? That accident could have been *way* worse, but we both walked away from it unscathed. Her insurance company paid for the repairs, and I was even able to get a few other dings buffed out at no charge—car detailing for free!

It's all about *perspective*.

I can also talk about all the times I focused on *good* things and had those things appear—making Varsity sports teams in high school; college acceptance letters and scholarships; a promising career with a bonus, 401K, and good health insurance; a company that paid for my Master's degree; an independent path to publish my books; buying a Mercedes (twice over); owning a 3,000 square-foot house on the lake; starting my own business and scaling it to six-figures in just one year's time; finally experiencing true freedom after leaving my corporate job . . .

But why does it seem like the bad always happens more often than the good? Because the emotion attached to the bad is *fear*. A huge, *huge* aspect of the Law of Attraction and Manifestation has to do with not just your thoughts, but also your feelings. Fear is an incredibly powerful emotion (and it can make people do crazy things!)—so when you simultaneously feel fearful and think negative thoughts, you're going to attract one giant dumpster fire into your life.

So many of us run on autopilot with fear-based thoughts every single day. We don't even realize we're doing it, and yet it's the one thing we have complete control over. It's the only thing we *need* to shift our perspective and see another version of our reality—the *better* version, where anything and everything is possible for you.

The main indicator of the victim mentality is the belief that things are constantly happening *to* you, when in reality, everything is happening *for* you—even the things you might perceive as bad. The underlying fear, then, is of loss—loss of self, loss of freedom, loss of time, loss of money—just *loss* in general. In always expecting the worst to happen and fearing that you'll lose something (whatever that something is), you never truly live. You're never fully present because you're fixated on the future—on the outcome.

I've known people who have stayed in relationships way past their expiration date because they're afraid of losing that person, that connection, that feeling of being loved—even if it's not being expressed by their partner anymore. I've watched friends and family members stay in jobs they hate because they're afraid to lose the security and stability that comes with a steady paycheck. I've witnessed insane diets and workout regimens and eating disorders because the fear of losing control outweighs a holistic view of health.

Let me make one thing very clear. **If you fear loss, you fear life itself.** We will inevitably lose things in this lifetime because our time here on this Earth is finite. We'll lose loved ones, material possessions, job titles, money, relationships, friendships, even our identities at times . . .

but if we never had to let go, would anything in our lives actually have meaning? If you knew that you would never die, would you appreciate life as much?

Loss creates vulnerability, and with that vulnerability comes an unparalleled sense of openness and exposure. If you're afraid of losing things, then how are you *not* afraid of the loss of what *could be*?

If I hadn't faced my fear of the unknown, I'd still be working in a job that sucked the life out of me.

If I hadn't faced my fear of judgment, I never would have connected with so many incredible people via my YouTube channel.

If I hadn't faced my fear of inadequacy and rejection, you wouldn't be reading this book right now (or any of my other books, for that matter).

Our lives are not meant to be a prison. We are not meant to live in fear, ignoring the callings of our hearts and settling for much, *much* less than we deserve. We all have such beautiful gifts to give this world—so much *soulflow* just waiting to be discovered—that it pains me to think that because of *fear*, only a select few will ever find the courage to start scaling that glorious mountain.

Victim mentality feeds off of fear. Every negative thought that enters your mind is **fuel** for manifesting the exact opposite of what you truly want. A surefire way to combat this is to shift your focus on what you can *gain*, instead of what you can lose. When you focus on what you can gain, then suddenly, the possibilities are endless.

Infinite opportunities await.

But only if you *think* they do—only if you *believe* it.

Love conquers fear. Abundance conquers fear. Gratitude conquers fear. When we attach these emotions to our positive thoughts, that's when the light can pour in—and faster than you ever could have imagined.

Playing the victim stops here. I want you to make that promise to yourself right now. From this point forward, everything that happens is happening *for you*—for your greater good. This book will require you to venture into a new level of self-awareness—one where you become fully aware of the thoughts you're thinking. Dare to ask the question, "What if this thought simply *wasn't* true?"

## Reflection

Review the beliefs you wrote down in last chapter's reflection. Carefully go through each one and ask yourself whether or not it's actually true. Is this belief the be-all, end-all . . . meaning you're absolutely certain, without a shadow of a doubt, that it's 100% true? Or is it possible that it's just based on the perception of those who introduced you to it in the first place? If you find that it isn't actually true, or you've experienced something that contradicts it, rewrite the story around that belief—one that feels more aligned with how you want to live your life.

# SOULFLOW

# *chapter three*

## THE OVERACHIEVEMENT SPIRAL

WORKING YOUR ASS off and reaching your goals is so, *so* satisfying, isn't it? Nothing gives me a greater sense of accomplishment than setting a goal and then absolutely crushing it on every level. Where my Type-A friends at? I see you, boo.

I've been an overachiever ever since I can remember. The obsession started young. From getting good grades in school to enlisting the kids in my neighborhood to go along with my crazy ideas to joining every youth club under the sun, *overachiever* was my middle name. I loved the sense of pride and accomplishment I felt after completing a project—and I still do—but after thirty years of pushing, achieving, pushing some more, achieving some more . . . I realized something. Once again, I was chasing something that was fleeting.

Don't get me wrong. It's great to look ahead, to plan for the future, to set goals and have things you want to achieve in this one beautiful, precious life . . . but at what cost?

There is no doubt in my mind that my overachieving tendencies have greatly shaped my standards of discipline, perseverance, and overall outlook on life. In my experience, overachievers are naturally optimistic. Not entitled—because we know we have to work hard for what we want—but always optimistic about the outcome. Because we achieve time and time again, we're confident we can do it again . . . and again.

Overachievers are the people who make things happen *no matter what*. This is great when you have a sense of who you truly are, what you really want, and *why* you do the things you do—that being said, it's easy to lose sight of what's truly important. This results in just going after the *next* title, the *next* status, the *next* level of success, recognition, and what have you for the sake of being able to say, "Look at what I've accomplished. Look at everything I've done."

When we put too much stock in our goals and aspirations, again, we're placing a dangerous amount of value on the *external*. What happens *if* we don't achieve those goals and aspirations—especially on the (usually insane) timelines we've set for ourselves? We suddenly feel less than. Unworthy. Incomplete.

I want you to hear me, loud and clear.

*You* are not your goals. *You* are not your aspirations.

*You* are **so much more** than that.

I'll talk more about something I like to call *attachment syndrome* in later chapters, but the issue with being so hyper-focused on achieving your goals is that, most of the time, the timeline—and the goal itself—is completely out of our control.

Yes, you heard me correctly.

The number one pitfall of the overachiever is trying to *force* things to happen in a certain way at a certain time. When we're in such a forceful state, we can't possibly be in flow with the Universe and divine timing. We think we know best—*because we have goals and timelines, dammit!*—and so we push and push and push, and even though roadblocks keep popping up and everything seems to be going wrong, we *keep on pushing*.

What if, instead of pushing, we stopped for a second and asked, "What is this obstacle trying to teach me? Why is it being presented to me over and over again?" We get *so* impatient with the timing of it all that we don't even give divine guidance a chance to intervene and point us in the right direction. We just barrel forward, full speed ahead, until something related to that goal eventually blows up in our face—and it will *always* blow up in your face.

I can't even begin to count how many things I've tried to force. From friendships with certain "it" girls to Ivy League University admissions to relationships that weren't right for me to story ideas that needed a tad more grooming to straightening my naturally curly hair in order to fit society's standards of "beauty" . . . the list goes on.

The most important thing I've learned when it comes to trying to force your goals to take shape at a certain time is this: You're only keeping yourself from fully experiencing your natural state of being—your *soulflow*.

When we overachieve, we tend to put unnecessary pressure and unrealistic expectations on ourselves—and on our work—which then causes us to behave out of fear—we get anxious, frustrated, and panicked when things don't pan out the way we originally hoped they would.

Soulflow cannot exist when fear is in the picture. Soulflow can only exist in a state of love. It's a sense of inner calm when things get thrown off course. It's the emergence of faith when your world is crumbling and falling at your feet. It's that feeling of surrender when you realize you've done your part and must now trust in the unknown to deliver the missing pieces—the ones you *aren't responsible* for making happen.

Soulflow is everything that is *already* inside of you.

My breakthrough as an overachiever and perfectionist

occurred about a year ago when I enrolled in an online coaching program. It was in the very first module of that program that I had to come face-to-face with one of my greatest insecurities about my overachieving tendencies: the *why* behind it. Something undeniably powerful happens when you take a moment to ask the hard questions and really dig into your belief system—and the reasoning behind why you do the things you do.

In that module, I addressed the sense of burnout and exhaustion I'd been feeling at the time. I wrote down a list of all the reasons why I was exhausted—but they were only *surface level* reasons. I wrote things like "filming, editing, and uploading two videos a week" and "being in the process of writing and publishing two books" and "trying to keep up with my social life and volunteering commitments" and so on and so forth. In reality, I was just listing all of the things I was *doing* that contributed to that burnout and exhaustion. It seemed I wasn't willing to look at things on a soul level— on a level related to worthiness.

Until I did.

And it left me in a giant mess of tears.

As I began to go deeper, I was able to trace back my overachieving tendencies. Why I got good grades in school. Why I joined honor societies and took AP classes and participated in sports. Why I applied to Ivy League schools. Why I got a job in a corporate setting. Why I focused on promotions and new job titles, even though I *hated* the work I was doing . . .

It's because I was *rewarded* when I overachieved.

I got *attention* when I overachieved.

I received the highest *praise* when I overachieved.

I received *love* when I overachieved.

Read that last sentence again.

When I overachieved . . . I felt *loved.*

As a child, my mind equated achievement with being loved. You won't be loved if you don't succeed. You won't be loved if you don't get into this school, or that program, or fall into a certain line of work. You won't be loved if you follow another path other than the one that has been so carefully laid out for you your whole entire life.

You. Will. Not. Be. Loved.

Dagger to the freakin' heart, man.

For the thirty years I've been on this planet, I've placed my **worth** in overachievement. In my eyes, I was not *worthy* if I wasn't overachieving. This realization shattered my entire reality. A million questions entered my mind. If I wasn't an overachiever, then who was I? If this didn't define my worth, then *what* did?

Your worth cannot be defined by external sources.

It must come from within. Period.

And I know you've probably heard that phrase from all the life coach gurus and in all the self-help books you've read, but the *reason* it's said, over and over again, is because it's **the truth**. Your internal dialogue—the thoughts you think and the things you feel—shapes your external reality.

So if you're constantly telling yourself that you're not good enough, that you need to do *more*, that you'll only be proud when you make this much money or drive that kind of car or live in this kind of house . . . you'll be running in circles your entire life. You'll be chasing your own tail—but why?! Your tail is already *attached* to you. So is your soulflow. It's already inside of you, right now, at this very moment . . . you just haven't tapped into it yet.

Let me tell you why always looking ahead to the next thing isn't all it's cracked up to be. As someone who has written and self-published six (possibly now seven) bestselling books, lives in a 3,000+ square-foot house on the lake, drives a Mercedes-Benz, launched a business that earned over six figures within the first year, has consistent five-figure digital course launches, impacts over 60,000 beautiful souls on social media, and had the choice—and *chose*—to quit her full-time corporate job . . .

Nothing compares to your first major milestone.

Nothing compares to reaching that "first" dream.

You know—the one you thought was *impossible.*

For me, that was writing and publishing a book. Don't get me wrong, I still get giddy and excited and feel all the feelings whenever a book launch rolls around . . . but that feeling I had the very *first* time I did it? I will **never** have that feeling again—because your first time only happens once.

Same goes for when I hit my first 1,000 subscribers on YouTube. I was elated because I had hit that first "big" number, at least in my eyes. So when my subscriber count hit 5,000 . . . 10,000 . . . 20,000 . . . 30,000? You'd expect for that feeling to grow, right? But in all honesty, there really was no "next level" feeling. This isn't to say that I'm not grateful for all of the achievements after my "firsts"— of course I am! Each milestone I reach holds a special place in my heart, but not in the way you might think.

Over time, I've come to realize that my achievements do not *define* who I am as a person. Being a bestselling author does not define me. Being a six-figure creative entrepreneur does not define me. Being a writing and business success coach does not define me. These are all things I have accomplished, but again, they are external.

What I am . . . is love. Passion. Fire. Kindness. Empathy. Creativity. A light in an otherwise dark and cynical world. What I am . . . is *soul*. Deep down, I know that my achievements are not *me*. The shape of my body is not *me*. Hell, even the thoughts I think are not *me*.

I get asked all the time how to write a book, how to start a business, how I manage my time, how to *insert writing/time management/productivity goal here*—and what I so desperately want to divulge is that accomplishments are **meaningless** unless the *why* behind them stems from the deepest desires of your soul.

If you think you'll finally "make it" and *feel* like a "real writer" only after hitting the New York Times Bestsellers List . . . think again. You became a "real writer" the minute you wrote the first damn sentence of your manuscript. If you think you'll finally be considered a "successful entrepreneur" after earning six figures . . . think again. You became a "successful entrepreneur" the moment you decided to launch a product or service that will enrich the lives of others. If you think you'll reach the pinnacle of happiness once you have seven figures sitting in your bank account . . . think again. Your happiness cannot be measured by monetary means—because your happiness is not contingent on *the external*.

What so many of us seem to miss is that it's not the thing itself you're hoping to achieve—whether it's a goal, a milestone, or some other achievement—it's the *feeling* you think it'll give you. For example, your goal to be a full-time entrepreneur is not so much about finally quitting your job and working for yourself—it's about the *feeling* of freedom, to design your days however you choose. What we don't realize is that those feelings are *already* inside of us—they're just waiting to be activated.

You want to feel free? Go on a spontaneous road trip next weekend. You want to feel pampered? Schedule a spa day, either at home or at a salon. You want to feel loved? Make love to yourself (oh yes, girl, I went there!).

**Stop waiting** for something external to swoop in and make you feel a certain way. You already *know* what these things will feel like because you're imagining that *x* will *give* you that feeling! Tap into that. Feel the feelings *right now*. There's nothing stopping you—so why are you waiting?

This is the largest misconception when it comes to setting goals. You don't have to achieve anything to feel the way you want to feel. You can feel *all* the feelings right now . . . you just have to be self-aware enough to do so.

## Reflection

What are your stories around achievement? Are you an overachiever at heart or was it, perhaps, by design? What does your overachievement result in? Does the constant striving for *more* lead to burnout and exhaustion? Imagine for a moment what your life could look like if you slowed down. And if you can't imagine this, I encourage you to take a day off to just *be*. The world won't come crashing down. Everything will still be waiting for you when you return. Trust me. Take some time to *be*, instead of *do*.

_____

_____

_____

_____

_____

_____

_____

_____

_____

_____

# SOULFLOW

# chapter four

## THE CONSUMPTION CYCLE

IN ALL HONESTY, I've been putting off writing this chapter because there's so much I want to say, and yet so much I want to keep to myself. In the last chapter, we talked about the concept of "wanting more" on an intangible level, so let's switch to the more tangible plane, shall we?

Consumption comes in many different forms. From overspending on shopping sprees to overindulging at the buffet to gambling, drug, and alcohol addictions to scrolling social media to marathoning your favorite binge-worthy Netflix Originals . . . sometimes it feels like all we do is *consume*.

Don't get me wrong—consumption isn't inherently good or bad. After all, it's how we stay informed within our communities, as well as on a global scale, connect with like-minded individuals, discover new things, and sometimes even find that much-desired inspiration. But have you ever stopped to ask yourself just how *much* you're consuming and, more importantly, exactly *what* that consumption entails?

Are you constantly watching news channels that strike the fear of God into you? Are you spending half your day scrolling through Instagram, comparing your life to everyone else's highlight reel? Are you re-watching every season of The Real Housewives of Beverly Hills for the fourth time? Are you reaching for that third glass of cabernet . . . on your second bottle? Like I said before, consumption isn't inherently good or bad—but consumption in excess? We might be leaning heavily toward the latter.

Real quick, I want you to make a list of everything you've consumed today—and if it's too much to keep straight in your head, then write it down. I'm talking the music you jammed to while getting ready this morning, the triple shot espresso you ordered in the Starbucks drive-thru, the podcast you listened to on your way to work, the hours you spent scrolling social media, emails, and news sites, the candles you bought at Bath and Body Works on your lunch break . . . *all* of it. Now circle (or mentally tick off) those items that are media-based (or information-based—and yes, that includes any type of e-learning through digital courses or programs). Now go through the list again and underline the things you *created*—and no, those twenty emails you sent at work today don't count.

For those who are at least *aware* that their soulflow exists, you may find that you actually did carve out a little time to create—maybe to write a blog post, or sketch something in a notebook, or write some words for a book project, or cook a meal from scratch. But for those of you who didn't underline anything . . .

When was the last time you created something? Painted? Sang? Wrote a story? Sculpted? Sketched? Played the piano? Strummed a guitar? Initiated a DIY project? Busted out the sewing machine? Took a photo that *wasn't* going to be posted on Instagram? When was the last time you built **something** from *nothing*?

The consumption cycle occurs when we spend *all* of our time consuming and little to no time creating. Even if you think that you don't have a creative bone in your body, I can almost guarantee that six-year-old-you would make a mud pie and fling said mud pie at your face.

Oh look, you *did* create something—a mud pie.

All joking aside, this is a serious epidemic.

As children, the world is our oyster. We don't spend as much time consuming because we're outside playing in the streets (although, sadly, with the rise of technology, I'm pretty sure this has changed). When I was growing up, the

Internet was just becoming a thing (oh, AOL dial-up) and so the way I spent my time was by playing outside with my friends and—you guessed it—creating. I created makeshift books out of printer paper and wrote my stories in them. I brainstormed plays and acted them out with my Barbie dolls and American Girl dolls. I made handwritten spelling and math worksheets that I used to teach the younger kids in my neighborhood. I made up new worlds, new languages, new "recipes", new games—creating, creating, creating.

Always creating.

As children, we are, in a sense, fearless. As adults . . . not so much. It's easy to see why our fearlessness fades as we grow up. We're introduced to responsibilities, and with those responsibilities come things like expectation.

Judgment. Comparison. Rejection. Societal pressures.

Fear. Fear. Fear.

We're introduced to *fear*—fear of being judged, compared, and rejected. We quickly come to realize, then, that when we consume, we *can't* be judged, compared, or rejected. So we play it safe by never creating. We stay small by solely consuming.

What we fail to realize is that by **only** consuming, we're allowing everything *else* to dictate how we live our lives. This newscaster says it's not safe to go outside, so you don't go outside. This fashion blogger says that if you don't own a pair of espadrilles, your wardrobe will die a slow death, so you buy a pair of espadrilles. This fitness guru says that if you don't drink *this* protein powder, you'll be destined to look like she did in her "before" photos (which were probably stunning to begin with!).

When exactly did we lose the ability to think for ourselves? Correction, let me rephrase that. When did we *choose* to stop thinking for ourselves? When did we *choose* to stop making our own decisions?

I'll tell you when. It was the moment you decided you'd rather pursue a life of mediocrity and "safety" than risk a life of creation, wonderment, and joy. It was the moment you decided to settle for less because you didn't think you were worth your big, crazy, totally "out there" dreams. It was the moment you decided—subconsciously or not—to snuff out your *soulflow*.

If you happen to identify with the level of consumption I've mentioned over the last few pages, please, *please* don't scold yourself. When you scold yourself, you judge yourself for doing something wrong. Judgment brings about feelings of shame. And when we feel ashamed, we turn to those vices that place a temporary Band-Aid over how we're feeling—shopping sprees, gambling, drugs, overindulging, et cetera.

Overconsumption ultimately stems from the fear of not having enough. Deep down, you don't *really* buy that new purse because it's trending—you buy it because you believe it'll somehow provide validation that you have "enough".

You don't hoard items because they hold sentimental

value—you hoard them because *what if one day you need this particular size strainer even though you have four more and haven't used any of them in over a year?* Let go of the damn strainer, Susie.

You don't eat a tub of ice cream every single night before bed because you feel you deserve it after a day of eating clean and working out—you eat it because your feelings of inadequacy lead you to sabotage your goals. You don't believe you're *worthy* of being in shape and you expect yourself to eat that ice cream anyway, so that's what you end up doing.

You don't blow half of your savings on gambling for the chance to win it all back and then some—you gamble because, deep down, you worry that the money is going to run out eventually, but not if you can help it, right? You can *control* how much you put on that table and when to stop. But can you really?

The source of this fear? Of not having enough?

Lack of power and feelings of inadequacy.

We consume because it's something we *can* control. We have the choice to buy that new purse. We have the choice to keep or donate the items in our home. We have the choice to eat that entire tub of Rocky Road in one sitting. We have the choice to throw our money on that poker table. Whether you realize it or not, we over-consume because we're afraid that there's not enough—that *we're* not enough.

Ouch.

Let's talk about addiction for a minute. While I am fortunate enough to have never fallen victim to addiction, I've dated plenty of people who have. I can't even begin to imagine, nor understand, the intricacies of an addict's mind, but I *have* been involved on a level so profound, I wouldn't wish it on my worst enemy. Being the anchor that clings desperately to the sand, trying to keep the ship from floating away?

Yeah. That's been me. Many, *many* times over.

I've dated alcoholics. Gambling addicts. What some would call drug addicts (although they called it an "experimental" phase)—and the thing that was most difficult to come to terms with, as someone who has a *non-*addictive personality, is that these people were trying to fill a void that no external source could satisfy. No matter how much money they'd throw on the table, no matter how many times they'd hit that stupid bong, no matter how many designer watches they'd buy, no matter how many drinks they'd put on their tab . . . it was never enough.

And it will never *be* enough.

This is the reality of addiction.

It's painful to witness, and it's even more painful to watch someone you really care about succumb to their addiction—because there's always an aftermath. Alcohol changes people. Gambling changes people. Drugs change people. Sure, it may bring out your daring, adventurous, and risky side, but it almost always reveals a darker, more sinister, more *uncontrolled* side—which is ironic because these vices are supposed to make us feel *in control* when actually, the exact opposite ends up happening.

So yes, we overconsume because we fear there's not enough, but we also do it because feelings of inadequacy, on some level, cause us *pain*. Pain makes people do crazy things, doesn't it? Abuse, sexual assault, run-ins with the cops, life-ruining-or-threatening decisions—these are usually the types of things that result from unmanaged feelings of inadequacy. Sadly, what addicts can't seem to wrap their heads around is that their decisions not only affect their lives . . . they also affect the lives of those they care about most.

In college, I dated someone who was going through a pretty intense "experimental phase", specifically with drugs. Marijuana, cocaine, ecstasy, oxycodone . . . this "phase" continued even after he'd graduated. The worst part about being in a relationship with someone who's always high? I never actually got to know the "real" him because *he* didn't even know who that person was.

And that's the point I'm trying to make right there. In the throes of addiction, whether you're the addict or someone you care about is, addiction masks our true state of oneness—our soulflow. How can you get to know yourself if all of your time is spent consuming? Moreover, why would you even want to get to know yourself if you've already come to the decision that you're *not enough*?

Let's switch gears to another form of consumption. Overspending—a topic I know many can relate to. We'll start with a background of my spending habits. To be frank, I am an overspender through and through. For most of my life, I've lived beyond my means . . . until about a year ago. We'll get into that later, but for now, let's talk about my mindset pre-soul-awakening.

When I used to spend money, it was because I wanted *things*. Not experiences—but *things*. Like many of us, my spending behavior was driven by external factors. When I was a kid, I'd spend my allowance on the latest toys— Barbies, Tamagotchis, or American Girl accessories. When I was in middle school, I started to get into fashion and makeup. Buying the latest clear lip gloss (yes, that was a thing), or jeans with no back pockets (also a thing), or yet another tattoo choker necklace (which have somehow come back into style), and let's not forget the chunky Tiffany & Co. charm bracelets and necklaces—those I *really* had to save up for. In high school, designer jeans were all the rage—Seven jeans and Citizens of Humanity— especially if you had the bedazzled back pockets.

The point of taking you down memory lane is this: I used to spend money on things I *thought* would make me be perceived in a certain way. I bought things because all the girls at school had whatever that thing was, and not having it somehow made me "less than" them. I think many of us can relate to this mindset, even now as adults. We want the new car, the bigger house, the latest piece of technology—when, in reality, what we currently have is perfectly fine.

Media. Advertisements. Commercials. Our peers. We learn about the next great "thing" and suddenly we're all-consumed by it. We need it, we must have it. Now, now, now. And to no fault of our own. It's a consumer-driven society, this western culture. And I fell for it.

Until I found the way out.

I want to preface what I'm about to say with this: Wanting material things does **not** make you a bad person. Do I still get excited thinking about driving a Range Rover (my dream car) or one day living in a beautiful flat in London (my dream city)? Of course I do. But there's a difference—I'm not all-consumed by the need to acquire these things now, now, now.

I've had the 3,000 square-foot house. I've had the 15-foot pontoon boat. I've owned a Mercedes Benz—two, actually. I've had the Tory Burch bags, the Michael Kors wallets, and the Chanel sunglasses. I've had the Bobbi Brown, MAC, and Anastasia Beverley Hills makeup products. All before I turned thirty years old.

And you know what?

They're. Just. Things.

Joy from *things* is fleeting. It only lasts a short while. Two years into my 3,000 square-foot house? I wanted to downsize. I was tired of the yard work and constant mopping of the hardwood floors. A year into driving my

Mercedes? I was looking at Audi SUVs. Six months into owning the pontoon boat? I was so over the maintenance, extra insurance, and storage fees that I just wanted to be rid of the damn thing. And as for the designer brand clothes and accessories? The joy lasted maybe a week or so, but then I'd toss them to the back of my closet, only to be replaced by the "next" thing a week later.

It was *always* onto the next.

Here's the thing. There will always be "the next". Something new. Something better. Something improved. Consumerism has us so entangled in its web that we can't possibly break free. It just keeps spinning, and spinning, and spinning, so that we can't see the way out or through. The aftermath of overspending is awful—especially when you're using credit cards. A week of joy, a lifetime of interest and minimum payments. But even so, you still want MORE. Because more is better, right? More will make us happy. It just *has to*.

I knew that if I wanted to make a serious and lasting change when it came to my spending, I had to do the one thing I'd resisted doing my entire life. I had to look into my habits and identify what exactly was causing me to spend. I started calling these my **spending triggers**. And once I identified them, I was able to create an action plan to keep me from acting on said triggers.

The first spending trigger was obvious—media consumption. Seeing as Facebook and Instagram are inundated with ads nowadays, I couldn't scroll through my feed without seeing a personally targeted ad that was for something I undoubtedly wanted to buy. A new Erin Condren planner? Yep, need one. A Lululemon cycling towel? Absolutely. The latest FabFitFun box? Heck yes.

I knew what I had to do. If scrolling through social media triggered my spending habits . . . I needed to do it less. So that's exactly what I did. I set a designated "scroll time" on my phone and *consciously* scrolled—meaning I set a specific intention to **not** buy anything, to **not** click on any of the ads, no matter how enticing they might be.

My second spending trigger took a lot more internal digging. I knew I had to look even more closely at all the times I'd spent money in the past. Not just *what* I'd spent my money on—but what had been going on that day or week as well. I started by pulling up my bank statements from the month prior. I added up my expenses for each week, then cross-referenced with my day planner. I wasn't surprised to learn that almost all of my large expenditures came at a time when I was under a lot of pressure and stress.

Big presentation at work? How about I buy myself a new blazer that will (hopefully) boost my confidence?

Tension in my relationship? Suppose I'll treat myself to a spa day—facial, mani/pedi, hair appointment, massage— *the works.*

Decision fatigue in choosing the next book to read? Guess I'll buy another five books to add to my growing

TBR (to-be-read) list instead of reading one of the hundreds of unread copies sitting idly on my bookshelf.

It's okay. We've all been there.

**But get this:** my desire to spend money on these things wasn't actually the problem. The *problem* was that these triggers—the media, the stress, the pressure—were appearing in my life on a regular basis. Like, weekly.

Do I think it's wrong to spend money on a new piece of clothing you love or pamper yourself at the spa or add another book to your collection? Absolutely not! I still do *all* of these things—but there's one major difference between then and now. *Before*, I was spending solely to cope with my feelings. Instead of looking at my situation and identifying *which* areas were causing me the most stress, I simply glossed over them and went after a quick fix—and that quick fix just so happened to be buying *things*. I'd get that brief feeling of happiness from obtaining something new, only to find that I had to repeat the process the next week when the next high-pressure, high-stress situation rolled around. It's a vicious cycle—which is why I call it **the consumption cycle**.

Had I found the courage to explore deeper, to sit with the shadows and the darkness, to ascertain exactly *which* situations were causing me the most stress, and gather the strength to remove them from my life . . . perhaps I could have saved myself from a mountain of credit card debt, pointless loans, and a closet full of stuff I used only once or twice.

It's not *what* we're spending our money on—it's the behavior behind it. It's the *why*. Are you buying something because it's something you truly desire and know, in your heart of hearts, that, as something external, it won't fill the void? Or are you buying something as a way to cope with your feelings, to mask the reality of your situation with something shiny and new? These are very, *very* different behaviors, and it's absolutely crucial to be able to distinguish one from the other.

After discerning my *why* behind my spending, as well as ridding my life of toxic relationships, friendships, work settings, and basically anything that no longer served me, I found that my spending—my *consumption*—dramatically decreased. Nowadays, if I'm struggling with confidence or self-esteem, I don't go buy a new outfit . . . I meditate and journal through my feelings instead. If I'm feeling uneasy in a friendship or a relationship, I don't run away to the spa and drop a boatload of cash . . . I reach out to that person, start a conversation, and express what's been weighing on my heart. If I'm feeling indecisive, I no longer ignore what I already own by adding something new to the collection . . . I turn to gratitude and focus on all the things I *do* have versus what I don't.

I'm not saying it was easy for me to get to this point. It took a lot of time and a lot of internal work and a lot of energy to face the harsh truths I'd been hiding from all those years. But in doing so, I was able to recognize a pattern of behavior that wasn't aligned with who I truly was—one that was keeping me from experiencing my soulflow. Before, it'd almost felt as though I'd been rewarding myself for "dealing with" those toxic situations—with new clothes, spa days, and other material items—instead of addressing them in a way where I'd find lasting peace, forgiveness, and happiness . . .

By turning within.

Fear wants you to believe that you are not enough. That you need external things to feel worthy, to feel as though you've "arrived", to be accepted and approved of and loved. It wants you to stay in the consumption cycle for the rest of your life so that you'll never discover what's resided in you all along . . .

Wholeness. Joy. And love.

# Reflection

Consider your consumption habits. Are you constantly on the hamster wheel, mindlessly scrolling social media, or are you spending your time in a way that actively engages your creative side? Do you overspend? Do you go a little too far when taking part in recreational activities? Do you gamble? Pick three consumption habits you identify with the most and write them in the space below. Try to identify your triggers—what causes you to consume? Is it related to stress? Needing approval? Being bored? Feeling unfulfilled? Once you've identified your consumption triggers, write down three ways in which you can combat it. When stress or approval or boredom strike, what will you do instead of consuming?

_____

_____

_____

_____

_____

_____

_____

_____

_____

_____

_____

_____

_____

_____

_____

_____

_____

_____

_____

_____

_____

_____

_____

# chapter five

## THE JUDGMENT DISORDER

IN MY FIRST personal development book, *Be Your Own #Goals*, I had an entire chapter dedicated to the dangers of comparison, so it only seemed fitting that I include its sister-chapter in this book—on judgment.

The world we now live in is a breeding ground for comparison and judgment, thanks, in large part, to the rise of technology and the Internet. With the touch of a button, social media has made it possible to share the highlights—our accomplishments, wins, and proudest moments . . . but it seems to be at the expense of our self-worth.

My judgment disorder started young, in fifth grade. I distinctly remember envying a girl's unparalleled beauty, sense of style, and rising popularity. As the tomboy with frizzy hair and glasses (oh judgment, my old friend), I wanted a taste of that kind of acceptance. I mean, who wouldn't?

One day, this girl wore a pair of blue jean overalls with a rainbow-striped shirt underneath to school (it was the 90s in Indiana). Overalls? Now *that's* something tomboy-Kristen could get behind. The dresses and skirts? Not so much. But overalls? Heck yes!

Every time I passed her in the hall, I couldn't help but notice her outfit. I also couldn't help but notice the way people fell at her feet, complimenting her and wanting to walk with her to class. So what did I do when I got home that day from school? I asked my mom if we could go shopping. Mind you, we'd just gone back-to-school shopping, but my mom was such a team player when I was growing up that she agreed. I had a feeling I'd find a way to satiate my outfit-envy by shopping at Limited Too (trying *so* hard not to date myself here!)—and, sure enough, I did. In fact, I found the exact *same* outfit.

I'm sure you can sense where this is going . . .

*Oh no, Kristen. Oh no you didn't!*

Oh yes. Yes I did.

Overjoyed, I hastily pulled the rainbow-striped shirt and overalls from their hangers, ran into the first open curtain-covered stall, and tried them on. I'm sure my mom was thinking the entire time that this wasn't my style *at all*, but again, as a team player, she bought the outfit for me anyway. Pink and purple bag in hand, we made for the parking lot and headed home.

How I wish that were the end of the story, but alas, it isn't. I waited quite some time (a week, which is forever when you're a ten-year-old) to wear that outfit to school. And you know what happened the day I did? She wore hers *again*. Cue curling up into a ball in adamant refusal to leave my bedroom for the foreseeable future.

As females, for some reason, we have this unspoken judgment that wearing the same thing as another woman is shameful. I don't know how this thought percolated or why it's stuck around all these years, but whether it's a chance accident or on purpose (like my situation), for most, it's pretty high up on what I like to call the *oh shit list*.

Especially at weddings, I've recalled so many occasions where two women who were wearing the same dress pretend to laugh it off and take photos together the entire evening, suddenly becoming besties—except they're not because it's all just an act. I know this because of the many curt conversations I've accidentally stumbled on in the bathroom during said weddings.

Ladies, *why* do we do this? Why does it even matter? I can promise you that it's not a big deal—it's only a big deal if you make it one. No one's going to remember the dress debacle of 2015 except for you . . . and maybe your new "bestie".

Just sayin'.

I digress. Back to my fifth-grade drama.

Seeing as my wearing the exact same outfit *wasn't* a chance accident, I knew I'd be in for a real treat. Because everyone had seen *her* wear it first, I was undoubtedly the copycat. And I was. I wholeheartedly admit to that. I liked her outfit, so I bought the same one.

Fortunately, this girl was extremely nice and we ended up becoming very close friends that day, especially when I learned that she lived in my neighborhood. She wasn't mean or cruel or condescending about the fact that I'd copied her, and she certainly didn't make a big deal about it. To her, it was just another day at school. And since she was okay with it—and *showed* that she was okay with it—everyone else just so happened to be, too.

I didn't know it back then, but what people were drawn to had absolutely nothing to do with her outfit. It was her self-assurance. Her confidence in who she was. And, I must say, for a fifth-grader, that's pretty mature (and admirable) behavior. From what I could gather, she didn't waste time with comparison or judgment—there was no "who wore it better", no *copycat* mentality on her end. We were just two girls at school who happened to be wearing the same outfit.

Did I feel somewhat embarrassed that day? Yes. Did I judge myself for it? Yes—although I was too young to understand that that's what I was doing. Up until that point, I'd been taught that copying others was shameful, that you should always aim to be original and think for yourself. To some degree, I agree with this. But, as with everything in life, there *is* a balance here.

Yin and Yang.

Now I'm not saying that you should copy someone flat-out (like I did with that outfit) or plagiarize work that isn't yours. If it's not yours, don't try to take credit for it. But to draw inspiration from things that speak to you? That's perfectly okay in my book. In fact, I believe it's absolutely necessary in order to tap into your soulflow.

Consider this for a moment. Who would the writer be without her muse? What would the vocalist sing about if not for the songwriter's poetry? What would the painter brush across his canvas if not for the rolling hills of Tuscany? What would the chef cook if not first experiencing dishes from all over the world?

All art is *inspired.*

All creation is *inspired.*

We talked about consumption versus creation in the last chapter, specifically why and how we should endeavor to create more than we consume. Creating something from nothing can lead to pride, achievement, and new opportunities . . . but it can also lead to doubt, judgment, and comparison.

We may not realize it, but so much of who we are and what we do longs to be kept within—but somehow, through our egos and what have you, always ends up outside of ourselves. What do I mean by this?

The times when I'm happiest and truly tapped into my soulflow aren't when I'm responding to comments on my YouTube videos, launching digital courses and programs, or releasing books into the world . . .

It's when I'm completely and utterly alone with my art.

When I am truly *one* with my art.

It's in the brainstorming and mind mapping for my next book; the nitty gritty of building the modules for future self-study programs; the actual typing of the words on the screen (what I'm doing at this very moment as I sit on an airplane headed to Phoenix). But the moment that program is launched? Or that video is posted? Or that book is published? That's the space where it shifts from being *my art* to being *content*.

This isn't to say that I'm not insanely thankful for my tribe, my fans, my viewers, my platform, for those of you reading this book right now. Because I **am**—and it's to a degree that cannot even be put into words. It's because of you that I am able to do what I love for a living, and for that, I am eternally grateful.

That shift though, from art to content, is where soulflow begins to wither as doubt swoops in to take its place. Suddenly, your art—your *creation*—is out there for everyone to judge, review, criticize, and compare. It's also there for people to admire, appreciate, praise, and reward.

Want to know what's sad about that last sentence I just wrote? I had no problem coming up with all the negative things people do when it comes to art—like judging, reviewing, criticizing, and comparing—but when it came to the positive stuff? I had to highlight the word *praise* and click "Find Synonyms" in the drop-down menu. If you could see me right now, I'm shaking my head.

Why is it that, when it comes to music, books, movies, artwork, or any other *creation*, people have this uncivilized urge to try to rip it apart? Why do we always look for the bad? Why do we compare this movie to that one? Why do we attempt to dismantle an author's plot before the entire series has been released? Why do we stoop so low and say things like, "Oh, I love that song, but I can't stand Taylor Swift"? (And I'm just using that as an example because I'm a total Swiftie!).

What is it about human nature that makes us so prone—and so *drawn*—to judge and compare? At first, I thought it would be a complex answer, one that would require a lot of research, analysis, and—get this—*comparison*, when in fact, it's really quite simple.

It's because of a lack of acceptance.

That's it. No bells and whistles. No fancy terminology.

At some point in our lives—as a child, adolescent, or perhaps later on in adulthood—we face some form of **rejection**. We're told we aren't good enough, aren't strong enough, aren't pretty enough, aren't smart enough, aren't capable enough . . . aren't *enough* in general.

Are we sensing a pattern here?

We all handle rejection in different ways. For some,

rejection is a brutal slap in the face that ceases all future pursuit of their hopes and dreams. For others, the lifetime of rejection gets buried underneath the surface and results in unmanaged pain, which then manifests in its own pit of darkness, despair, and insecurity—what we know today as gossip columns, many news cycles, trolls, haters, and the like. But, for a select few (like me), it lights a fire under their ass because ain't nobody gonna tell them what they can and cannot do. Someone else's judgment of your work, your art, your *creation* **does not matter**. What they compare it to **does not matter**. What they say in their review **does not matter**.

Art is subjective.

It always will be.

*And*, if not for the courageous, beautiful souls in this world who create—who bring you movies and books and art and music and *entertainment*—just what would you do with your time? Honestly? Die of boredom? There would be nothing to consume. Nothing to judge. Nothing to compare. Nothing to criticize. **Anyone** can consume, but it takes a very courageous individual to *create*.

The only people you should take advice from are those playing in the same arena—those who have skin in the game—because *those* people actually know what the hell they're talking about. If I took advice from every reader and every book review, guess what? Every single one of my books would be riding the hot mess express. They'd be unrecognizable. They wouldn't be *mine* anymore. I don't know about you, but I'd rather have something be wholly, irrevocably mine, even if that means getting thousands of bad reviews. At least I *did* something. I took an idea and created something from nothing. I had the courage to put myself out there. I *made* art. That's a hell of a lot more than most people can say for themselves.

Okay, I'll get off of my soapbox now.

(But really, that's something to think about.)

Back to judgment—*judgment* stems from lack of acceptance or, put more plainly, from rejection. Judgment *needs* you to be in this state of "lack" in order for it to not just survive, but **thrive**. In a twisted way, judgment is a defense mechanism, one that's trying to protect you from feeling hurt by people who don't *understand* you.

Facing rejection simply means that we aren't accepted. That we're misunderstood. This then leads us to thinking that we're not "enough". From that point forward, we see everything through a lens of "not enough"—and that lens can be pointed at ourselves *or* at other people. Or both. Our disappointment in our own failures and rejections leads us to look for faults in others. Looking for faults in ourselves, and in others, results in judgment. Envy. Comparison. Competition.

This pains me to admit, but I used to pass judgment on women who weren't financially independent, namely those that I referred to as "glorified housewives". Just typing that makes me feel all sorts of embarrassed, *but*, as someone who works tirelessly on her goals and *earns* that sense of achievement, I used to look down on those women who stayed at home, who didn't have to go to work, who didn't have to worry about making a living. I thought that they were lazy, that they'd taken the easy way out, and that they'd never know accomplishment the way a hustler (like me) would.

Harsh, right?

Until I realized something that shook me to my core.

I *envied* these women.

And what I envied about them . . . was their *freedom*.

Their days were whatever they wanted them to be. They could be filled with cooking, baking, and cleaning or brunching, exercising, and reading . . .

Or writing a book.

Or building a business.

Or impacting others.

Ding ding ding. My, doesn't that sound familiar?

Deep down, I'd always desired the **freedom** to spend my time however I wanted. But I'd spent most of my life studying in school, pursuing higher education, on a path to start a booming, successful career that would help me become financially independent. That was *my* journey. So just because someone was handed a trust fund or happened to marry someone wealthy doesn't make their path any less valid.

It's just **different**.

Our judgments have a way of signaling to us what it is

we truly desire. If you find yourself judging another woman's bold outfit choices, perhaps it's because you wish you had the courage to wear the neon leggings and leopard jacket that are currently collecting dust in your closet. If you find yourself judging someone for following their passions, perhaps it's because you wish you'd taken the time to discover passions of your own. If you find yourself judging anything, for any reason, perhaps you should ask yourself *why* that thought appeared in your mind in the first place.

What nudge is your judgment trying to give you?

If left unchecked, judgment will run your life. Envy and jealousy will eat you alive. Comparison will breed competition. Ultimately, you'll find yourself criticizing all the people who are doing the very things you *wish* you had the courage to pursue.

Hatred will get you absolutely nowhere.

*Fear* will get you absolutely nowhere.

Listen, there's enough room for everyone at the table. There's enough room for your books and your friend's books and that other girl's books, for indie books and traditionally published books. There's enough room for this style of coaching and that style of coaching. There's enough room for this fitness program and that strength-training regimen. There's enough room for gluten-free, sugar-free, *and* vegan cupcakes.

There. Is. Enough. Room.

The Universe is infinite, a never-ending platter of individual expression and a buffet of endless options. No one and nothing is perfect. And guess what? If you don't vibe with something, you don't have to consume it. It's completely your choice. At the end of the day, we're all just doing our best. Your judgment might say that that's not good enough, but **it is**.

You just have to decide that it's good enough *for you*.

## Reflection

When was the last time you passed judgment, whether out loud or in your head? Was it at the café when a woman burst through the doors, balancing a cell phone in one hand and a stroller in the other? Was it when you wrote that last chapter, read through it, and decided that you were the worst writer on the planet? Was it in a hurtful comment you left online or in an overly critical review? Reflect on that. How did it make you feel in the moment? How do you feel right now?

Tearing others (and ourselves down) only dims the light in this world. If you find that you pass judgment on a regular basis, work on pinpointing what form of past rejection that particular judgment stems from. When were you made to feel like you weren't "enough"? How did that make you feel? . . . And *why* would you want to make anyone else feel that way? You have a choice: Your words can either plant gardens or burn whole forests down. Use the space below to write five things you admire about yourself, and five people you admire and why—then email those people or comment on their social media accounts and let them know how they've impacted you.

_____

_____

_____

_____

_____

_____

_____

_____

_____

_____

_____

_____

_____

_____

_____

_____

_____

_____

_____

_____

_____

_____

_____

## chapter six

### THE ACCEPTANCE CONUNDRUM

ACCEPTANCE HAS NEVER been an easy topic for me to breach. I'd be lying if I said that this wasn't the fifth rewrite of this opening paragraph—and this entire chapter, for that matter.

Acceptance is something I've struggled with for most of my adult life, except I never would have admitted that *that's* what it was. But for so many years, I did things because it was "accepted" in the eyes of others.

The norms of society.

The status quo.

And as much as I'd sit there and say, "I don't care what other people think about me" . . . ultimately, I did.

Ultimately, I still do.

Look, we're human. It's logical to want to be liked. It makes sense to crave a sense of community and belonging. To discover the power of connection with fellow human beings. But what happens when you're *not* accepted? When you feel like an outsider? When you feel like no one truly understands you and, even worse, isn't willing to give you a real chance?

If you had asked me a year ago if I'd considered myself a people-pleaser, I would have rolled my eyes and scoffed. "Of course not. I don't care what people think about me." *Denial much?* Raise your hand if a similar phrase has ever left your mouth.

As human beings, acceptance is wired into our psychology. Ever heard of Abraham Maslow? What about Maslow's Hierarchy of Needs? According to this theory, there are five levels of needs that we, as human beings, require: *physiological* needs, like breathing, food, water, and sleep; *safety* needs, like security of body, employment, resources, morality, the family, health, and property; *love and belonging* with family, friendships, and intimate relationships; *esteem* including confidence in oneself, achievement, respect of others, and respect by others; and *self-actualization* including morality, creativity, spontaneity, problem solving, lack of prejudice, and acceptance of facts.

This basic need to belong, to feel accepted—it doesn't make us weak or superficial or selfish. It's okay to want to be liked. It's okay to want strong, genuine relationships. It's okay to *love* and to want to be loved in return. Where we tend to find ourselves in what I like to call the *acceptance conundrum* is when we begin to value the opinions, ideals, and morals of others **more** than our own.

Let me ask you something. When was the last time you did something because *you* wanted to do it? Not because it would make your parents, spouse, or boss happy, but because it would make *you* happy?

Let me ask you another question. In the last week, how many times did you act on something simply because it was expected of you? As a mom, as a student, as a partner, as an employee, as a business owner—how many of your choices on a daily basis revolve around what *others* will think about it? If I had to guess, it's probably a lot. Probably the majority.

I get it. You have a life, and with that life comes responsibilities. But how many of those responsibilities fall under the umbrella of acceptance? Of needing approval from other people? Of needing permission?

Do you bake two hundred gluten-free, sugar-free, dairy-free cookies for your kid's school bake sale because *you* want to, or because that's the "acceptable" course of action as a mom? Do you work overtime on projects to meet deadlines because *you* want to, or because that's what's "acceptable" in the eyes of your boss? Do you drop everything the minute a friend or family member needs you because *you* want to, or because that's what's "acceptable" as a friend/sister/cousin/daughter-in-law?

Yikes. I know that last one probably made you think, "Did she really just say that?" And yes, I did, so that I could make this point: If it's something you *truly* want to do—if it's something that stems from a core *desire*—then get after it! Bake those two hundred cookies, stay late to finish that project, go to the fifth brunch that month at your mother-in-law's. But please understand that there's a *major* difference between doing something from a place of true desire and doing something because it's "expected" or what's "acceptable".

Approval, acceptance, needing permission . . . no matter how you frame it, you're still seeking something external. It's validation from *something* else—from other people, other situations, certain circumstances—and in order to wade out of this murky pond of acceptance, you must be willing to set boundaries . . . and not "acceptable" boundaries in the eyes of others, but acceptable boundaries to **you**.

Because the term *boundary* can be easily misconstrued to focus on just the emotional side of things—like not allowing your kids to talk back to you because you expect a certain level of respect—I like to view boundaries as *minimums*. I define a **minimum** as a certain level that you're not willing to operate below.

Whether we realize it or not, we've all set minimums in our lives. Our living situations, how much money we make, how we're treated in relationships . . . minimums have been set. It's the *standard of living* that you're willing to accept.

Maybe you have a minimum around always paying your credit cards on time. What about taking at least one vacation a year? Or never being tardy to class? Or never letting your bank account dip below a certain number? Or starting the week off with a clean house and laundry put away? Or keeping the spark alive in your marriage by scheduling one date night a week?

Minimums are great because, on some level, they give us peace of mind and comfort. Operating at or above these minimums tells us that we're "doing life right". We accept ourselves, thereby signaling to others to accept us as well.

But have you ever stopped to consider just where these minimums and boundaries came from? Did you set them yourself, or were they carried over from past experiences?

When I first started building my online platform, I had a minimum around how much I shared about my personal life—in that the boundary was essentially nonexistent. I openly discussed many facets of my life, from my relationships to my full-time job to my daily lifestyle and routines. I documented family vacations and trips, conferences and events, and basically everything under the sun via video logs (also known as vlogs). I did this because I wanted to document my journey in pursuing my passion and becoming an author and creative entrepreneur—but I honestly didn't think it would grow to the size it is today.

Within a couple of years, I had tens of thousands of

people who knew who I was, how I lived my life, where I lived, what I did for work, and so on. I don't regret a single step of my journey, but had I realized the potential of my online platform early on, I probably would have set different boundaries around what I shared and didn't share. It's hard to fathom what it feels like to have complete strangers know the most intimate details of your life—and while the connection aspect has been nothing short of wonderful . . . at some point, I had to protect my energy.

And so my minimums—my *boundaries*—changed.

As things change and we evolve, our boundaries will also change and evolve. I'm more cognizant of what I share on my platform and the potential implications in doing so. I encourage you to look at every area of your life and identify what boundaries you have in place, what your minimums are, and where they came from.

Do you start the week off with a clean house because it's what you truly want to do, or because your mother told you that that's what a good housewife does?

Do you pinch and save every last dollar, even though you have a decent amount in your savings account, because it makes you feel secure, or because your financial advisor told you that your future depends on it?

Do you stay at your job because you truly love it, or because "that's what a responsible adult does"?

Once you identify your minimums and where they originated from, you may come to the realization that everyone *but you* had a part in writing the rules for your life. These rules, boundaries, and minimums you hold so dear—this acceptance conundrum—is nothing more than a façade . . . a perception of someone else's reality.

So *why* are you living in that reality? When did you decide that this was acceptable *for you*? Did you ever?

The root of the acceptance conundrum is lack of self-love or, put another way, lack of self-acceptance. If you don't love yourself—if you don't accept yourself for everything that you are—of course you're going to feel rejected. Of course you're going to feel inadequate. If you speak poorly to yourself, think self-deprecating thoughts, and use sarcasm as a way to communicate, then you're setting a minimum for how other people should treat you. If you don't treat yourself with love, kindness, and compassion, how can you expect other people to?

In my life, I have, what I consider to be, a close relationship with someone who struggles with acceptance. I see the emotional burden she carries. The constant worry on her face. The overanalyzing of every situation. The paranoia that others are always judging her. It's hard for me to really categorize this relationship as "close" because her self-expression is so limited that it might as well be closed off entirely.

Try as I might to ask the right questions, I get one-word answers. Try as I might to ask for advice, I get merely a shoulder shrug and a long bout of silence. Try as I might to express my feelings and emotions, I'm met with an exaggerated eye roll and a sarcastic tone.

Perhaps this relationship isn't "close" at all.

When we lack self-love, we lack self-acceptance. We don't express our opinions because we don't want to rock the boat. We settle because going after what we really want might upset this person or disappoint another. We never truly open up because it's "safer" to keep everything in.

The cost?

Isolation, alienation, and possibly even depression.

How ironic. The thing you fear, this lack of acceptance, is the very thing you'll end up getting if you listen *to* that fear. Your actions will result in discord. And what's worse is that because your soulflow is tethered to self-love—because they are inherently connected—one cannot be experienced without the other.

To need acceptance is to fear rejection, and yet facing and overcoming rejection is crucial in reclaiming your self-love. It's a catch-22. Self-love is required in order to experience soulflow—to experience your true state of being. Your oneness.

I haven't come across a single person who *hasn't* felt rejected, judged, not good enough, or misunderstood at some point in their lives. It's almost too easy to take these feelings to heart—and that's exactly what fear wants you to do. It's trying to keep you "safe" from potential hurt, but in doing so, it limits your experiences. It keeps you from *living* your life.

Just as art is subjective, so is rejection. Okay, so there's someone out there who said *no* to you, doesn't like you, or doesn't understand you. So what? Who *is* that person anyway? What makes *them* qualified to assess **your** worth? And why do you care so much about their opinion? If I had to guess, this person is probably a complete stranger.

I've lost count, but there are so many emails I've sent and applications I've submitted to speak at conferences and events that have been rejected. When I first queried *The Alpha Drive*, my debut novel, I received numerous rejections. Over the course of my life, I've heard the word *no* more than I've heard the word *yes*. And you want to know something?

That *excites* me.

It excites me because it's the Universe's way of nudging me in the right direction. It's a *signal* that I get to try another route, open another door, create a new opportunity—one that is better aligned with my life path and soul purpose.

Instead of fearing rejection . . . I embrace it.

If those Ivy League schools hadn't rejected me, I never would have gone to Arizona State University, which just so happened to inspire the setting in my debut novel, *The Alpha Drive*. If the company I worked for hadn't rejected me for certain promotions, I wouldn't have had the time to pursue writing my novels. If literary agents hadn't rejected those novels, I wouldn't have pursued self-publishing, which means my platform, as I know it, wouldn't be what it is today. Heck, it may not even exist.

I've created what I've created *because* of rejection. I've built an empire *from* that rejection. That is DAMN powerful, if you ask me. And so every time I hear *no*, it actually means *yes . . . yes* because something even better awaits.

Something I get to create.

I accept rejection as a part of my journey here on this Earth because it's inevitable. When I'm unsure of what's next, rejection steps in as divine guidance. Embracing rejection has led me to self-love because when you embrace rejection, you no longer look for external validation. Why would you when you accept yourself?

That's the *only* acceptance that actually matters.

As Eleanor Roosevelt once said, "No one can make you feel inferior without your consent." So stop hiding yourself for fear of being rejected or misunderstood. Take your power back. Protect your energy. Don't let others dictate what's acceptable to you, where you draw the line, what rules *you* want to play by. Write your own damn rules. You sure as hell don't need anyone's permission.

But deep down, you already knew that, didn't you?

## Reflection

In what areas of your life do you feel like you need permission, approval, or acceptance? Write down your current minimums in these areas and identify *where* these minimums came from. If it's an expectation someone else put on you, ask yourself if it's actually acceptable **to you**. If it's not, write a new minimum. Then write down the past rejections you've faced that have made you feel like you can't live your life the way you've always wanted. How have those rejections benefitted you? How will you commit to embracing rejection in the future?

_____

_____

_____

_____

_____

_____

_____

_____

_____

_____

_____

_____

_____

_____

_____

_____

_____

_____

_____

# SOULFLOW

# chapter seven

## THE ATTACHMENT SYNDROME

A T T A C H M E N T   is something I've struggled with for years . . . and for good reason. I think it's easy to become attached to a lot of things throughout our lives—identities, family members, friends, relationships, careers, thoughts, dreams, the *idea* of something or someone. I'm certainly guilty of holding on to things so tightly that I don't allow them to breathe, grow, or flourish.

For not leaving any room for the *magic* to happen.

I find that when I become attached to something, it's because I ultimately want to control it. I convince myself that if I follow these particular steps in this particular order that it'll give me *x* outcome. But what I failed to realize is that I was suffocating the already narrow pathway of inspiration.

Of soulflow.

Of *life*.

There is beauty in being detached. There is beauty in uncertainty. There is beauty in just letting things unfold.

My attachment syndrome started when I was in high school—I was attached (and obsessed) when it came to my body image. Although I was perfectly healthy and incredibly fit from all the sports I played, I had an overwhelming desire to be thin. This desire didn't come out of nowhere though. I didn't have a problem with my body until someone else *told* me there was one. I had never given a second thought to my muscular shape until other people at my school pointed it out. I even had a girl tell me, to my face, that some of the guys at school had said that I'd be more attractive if my ass wasn't "so ghetto." That statement carried into my adult years, and it stayed with me all through my corporate career, where I wouldn't dare leave the house without my long cardigan or blazer to cover my behind.

That was just one of many statements that led me down an insane path of fad diets, buying diet pills (which are horrific for you, by the way), over-exercising via two-a-days, binge-drinking in college and subsequent bulimia nervosa . . . I wreaked havoc on my body all because I grew an unhealthy attachment to an *idea* of how I "should" look.

An idea that *other* people had put into my head.

The problem with attaching to certain ideals, habits, people, or things lies in the level of fixation. To some degree, I'm sure we can all say we're a little attached to something, whether it's your job, your workout routine, your morning rituals, your brunch dates, your relationship, your hobbies, or something else. Don't get me wrong, it's great to give these areas of your life attention and develop discipline around habits and routines, but have you ever noticed that when you fixate too heavily on one area of your life, everything else seems to fall apart? Cue Nigel's oh so wise words from *The Devil Wears Prada*: "Let me know when your entire life goes up in smoke. That means it's time for a promotion."

Attachment is dangerous because it restricts the natural flow of our lives. On a subconscious level, it creates blinders—where we only see that *one* thing and nothing else. In neglecting the other areas of our lives, we send a signal to the Universe that it doesn't know what it's doing—that *we* know better. And I can tell you from personal experience that we most certainly DO NOT.

I can recall so many times where the moment I truly let go and stopped caring about something I was attached to was the *same* moment where that attachment suddenly just showed up out of the blue. This has happened with jobs, relationships, money, friendships, and pretty much *any* situation you can think of. I remember, for so many years, the times when I'd start dating again and I'd be so hell-bent on finding a boyfriend. My level of fixation was so high that I'd forego time with my girlfriends, my exercise routine, my hobbies and passions—basically, everything that made me *me*. How could I expect to find someone to be my partner when I wasn't even a partner to myself? How could I expect to meet someone as half the version of myself? Is *that* the person I want them to fall for? The one who doesn't take care of the things that are most important to her?

I think not.

But the minute I let go of "finding someone" and started treating the other areas of my life like the priority they were, a "someone" would fall right into my lap, completely unexpected.

Every. Single. Time.

This isn't to say that this "someone" was necessarily the right fit for me—the majority of the time, they weren't. And I've learned that's because I wasn't specific in who, or the type of person, I was trying to manifest and bring into my life. We'll never get what we don't have the courage to ask for.

Write that down.

Of course, if something isn't the right fit, it makes sense to let it go—but an unfortunate misconception of letting go is that it's the same as giving up. This is hardly the case.

Giving up is admitting defeat. Letting go, on the other hand, is releasing control of the situation . . . of the outcome. When we give up, we surrender the *why* behind the attachment. When we let go, we maintain the why, yet surrender to what *will be*—what will unfold naturally over time.

When I first started my entrepreneurial journey, I knew within weeks that I no longer wanted to work in a corporate setting. I knew the typical 9-5 desk job wasn't for me. I knew that being told what to do wasn't for me. I knew that what I needed every day was to do something I was crazy-passionate about—something where I could express myself freely without worrying what my colleagues (or anyone, for that matter) thought. And so I hustled—day in and day out—working long hours only to come home and work even longer hours (but those never felt like work because I was so in love with every facet of building my business).

As my business grew, I became overly attached to the idea of *when* I would finally quit my full-time job. It's great to have goals—but I took it to a level of fixation that wasn't healthy in the slightest. The thought of quitting wholly consumed me to the point where I would write updated resignation letters every couple of months. I became so obsessed with the "timing" of it all that I completely shut out my inner voice and intuition.

I abandoned my guidance system entirely.

I snuffed out my soulflow.

After a number of emotional breakdowns, tear-filled commutes home, and dim lights at the end of the tunnel after a toxic colleague or superior would leave, followed by an influx of inexperienced know-it-alls trying to tell me how to do my job, I found myself at a fork in the road.

Either I could continue to obsess over something that should have lit me up with excitement, but instead filled me with misery and shame because "it hadn't happened yet"; *or* I could surrender to divine timing. Not *my* divine timing, but TRUE divine timing. The *Universe's* timing. The timing that I couldn't, and shouldn't *want* to, control.

It was after a particularly grueling meeting with yet another "new" boss, with my head pressed against the steering wheel in the company parking lot, that I finally surrendered. The agony of trying to force something was just too much. I relinquished all control—I was so tired of feeling defeated that I wanted nothing to do with the decision anymore.

And that's when the realization hit me. I'd forgotten my why—*why* I'd wanted to quit in the first place. The fixation on the timing had pulled me so far away from the reason behind it that all I could see was the date on a calendar.

So I went back to my **why**.

My goal has, and always will be, to inspire people to be the truest version of themselves. To break out of the mind-numbing box society tries to force you into. To recognize that you are worthy of your deepest desires and that everything *can* and *will* happen for you, if only you'd just take a chance on yourself.

When I got back to my why, I was able to let go of the

timing. I didn't give up on the idea of quitting; rather I *let go* of my attachment to it. I released it *and* its hold on me.

Sure enough, just weeks later, divine timing stepped in and I quit my job.

In order to tap into our soulflow, we must release our attachments. If something isn't happening for you, take a look at where your focus is and what you're currently fixating on. Are you showing up every day with a grateful heart and trusting that everything will happen exactly the way it's supposed to? Or are you suffocating your dreams and desires with unreasonable demands and blocking any potential blessings from entering your life?

Attachment comes in many forms. Sometimes, we may not even realize that we have them, especially when it comes to our identities. I identified so heavily with being a professional working woman (because for a decade, it's all I'd known) that it's no wonder my timing didn't line up with that of the Universe's. How could I possibly expect to leave something behind that was such an integral part of the person I'd become? I hadn't surrendered it yet. Once I realized this, I knew I had a lot of work to do. It took a lot of time and effort to detach from this "corporate identity" I'd grown so attached to over the years.

Attachment to an identity can be debilitating because, once again, we're placing value in something outside of ourselves. Our identities provide a sense of validation. A sense of *worth*. If not for your identity—who you *think* you are—who would you be?

This is where the soul comes in. When someone asks us about ourselves, our response usually includes a long list of what we've done. I'm a health practitioner, a homeowner, a member of this and that organization. I'm a teacher, a mom, a wife. I'm an author, a business owner, a mentor. It never even crosses our minds to say something like, "I am love. I am humility. I am compassion. I am courage." . . . Because we don't even know what those things really mean.

We don't take the time to discover who we truly are.

The fear at play? Loss of self . . . but how can you "lose yourself" when you don't really know who you are to begin with?

Loss of self—or, in some cases, never getting to know oneself—ensues when there's been a consistent lack of self-expression. Feeling as though you can't express who you truly are can happen for a number of reasons, many of which we've already discussed in previous chapters.

To overcome any fear, we must pinpoint the exact moment (or moments) we were first introduced to that fear. When was the first time you tried to express yourself and felt unsupported? Misunderstood? Taken advantage of? Can you see how that moment may have caused you to unknowingly attach to an identity or ideal that wasn't actually true to who you are at your core?

Detachment requires surrendering.

And surrendering requires forgiveness.

This is why so many of us stay attached. To surrender something means it's no longer ours. It's no longer a crutch. It's no longer an excuse. Surrendering makes us vulnerable, and being vulnerable is hard. It means we're opening ourselves up to feel. It means we're susceptible to the darkness and the shadows, the hurt and the unmanaged pain from all those years of hiding.

But that vulnerability?

*That's* where soulflow can finally breathe.

It's only when we surrender who we *think* we are that we can finally become who we've always been.

What are you holding on to? What are you clinging to so tightly that letting go feels like accepting defeat? What in your life is desperately gasping for air? And why won't you let it *breathe*?

It could be your finances. Your kids. Your partner. Your job. Your passion. Your goals. Your aspirations. Your identity. You can sit here all day and name everything outside of yourself, but the key thing these all have in common is that they **stem** from *you*.

Start to ask *why* you're afraid of **the loss**.

Why are you afraid to lose control of your finances? Because it makes you vulnerable. Why are you helicopter-parenting and not allowing your kids to make their own decisions? Because it makes you vulnerable. Why are you afraid of losing your job? Because it makes you VULNERABLE.

I'm here to tell you that it is *okay* to be vulnerable. It is *okay* to let go. It is *okay* to be uncertain.

Surrender your fear of loss.

Detach from your attachments.

By staying attached, you're inviting the external to govern how you think, how you behave, how you *live*.

Soulflow doesn't live in the external.

So let go . . . and let live.

## Reflection

Use the space below to identify five things you're attached to. Do you gain anything by holding on to these things so tightly? What are you neglecting by fixating on just these areas? Are there any defining moments from the past that led you to attach to these things? Try to imagine letting go of the reins a little. Let these areas breathe. How different would your life look? What neglected areas could you then tend to? Surrender the control. Detach. Open your mind to another way—the *soulflow* way.

_____

_____

_____

_____

_____

_____

_____

# chapter eight

## THE GUILT COMPLEX

I USED TO feel guilty for flying first class, which is actually quite comical since I'm writing this current chapter in my first class seat. Tie it back to self-worth, not believing I was "good enough", or what have you, but I used to believe that the people who flew first class were wasting money—splurging on something completely unnecessary. Flying from Houston, specifically, you can get almost anywhere in three hours or less. I used to think . . .

*What's a few short hours of your life sitting in coach?*

*Why not spend that money on something else?*

That is, until someone very dear to me said something so profound, it nearly knocked me off my feet:

"What is three hours of your time *worth*?"

That question changed everything for me, especially after I became a full-time creative entrepreneur. What is my time *worth*? Lordy, where do I even begin?

I have books to write. YouTube videos and podcasts to brainstorm. Programs and courses to create. A **business** to run. Deadlines to meet—and yes, those deadlines may be self-imposed, but as an entrepreneur, you absolutely have to hold yourself accountable if you want to be successful.

Want to know how much work I get done while I'm sitting in coach? How many words I'm able to write? Maybe 300—and that's on a good day, you know, when no one's sitting in the middle seat. How many words will I write by the end of this 2 hour and 2 minute first class flight? I'll let you know by the end of this chapter, but you and I both know it'll be a hell of a lot more than 300 words.

We cannot (and should not) place a dollar value on our time. Sadly, it's the one thing we can't get more of. More money? Absolutely. More freedom? Yes indeed. But more time? Nope.

I'm sure you've sensed a pattern throughout this entire book. Worth, worth, worth. Your soulflow is innately tied to your sense of self-worth. What it all really comes down to is what *you've* decided that looks like.

It's your priorities.

Your non-negotiables.

As an entrepreneur, that looks like flying first class

whenever I can. Staying at 5-star resorts on international *and* domestic vacations. Owning a luxury vehicle. Buying organic produce on a weekly basis and eating at high-end restaurants whenever I get the urge. Living in a beautiful home with a naturally lit office, surrounded by as many books and plants as I can get my hands on. Reading as often as my schedule will allow. Learning new skills and trying new things. Riding my Peloton daily. Booking massages twice a month. Getting weekly manicures and pedicures. Saying no to the things I don't want to do, and saying yes to the things I really, *really* want to do. Spending quality time with family and friends as the best possible version of myself.

My **true** self.

How can I be the best version of myself if I'm behind on my business or my deadlines? How can I truly be present with my family and friends when all I'm thinking about is the fact that I only wrote 300 words in coach on the way to visit them?

The answer's simple. I can't be.

What is your time *worth*? Once you determine what that looks like, you'll be more inclined to make choices that are aligned with that level of worth. It took a long time for me to get over my guilt complex when it came to buying first class tickets. Usually, the first question that arises whenever I get off the plane is, "How was your flight?", to which I smile because I no longer have "horror stories". All of my flights are exceptional.

Because I **chose** for them to be that way.

Everything is a choice—*our* choice—and yet we worry about how those choices will be perceived. Do any of my family members run a creative entrepreneurial business? No. Should I expect them to understand how precious those three hours on that plane are? No. And I don't. There's no room for guilt when your choices are aligned with the best version of yourself, whatever that may look like for you.

It goes without saying that guilt is inherently tied to the concept of self-worth—to what you think you *deserve*. If you're anything like me, I love a good Netflix and chill sesh. Knowing that my couch, oversized pillows, and fuzzy blankets are patiently awaiting my arrival . . . I'm convinced there's nothing better after finishing up a long day—but that's just the problem. Why does it always *have* to be after a long day?

The guilt complex can manifest in many different forms, but for me, the art of "doing nothing" makes me feel all sorts of guilty . . . unless it comes after a long day.

Unless I feel like I *deserve* it—which isn't often.

Earlier in this book, you read all about my overachieving tendencies and where the belief about my worth being tied to achievement stems from—but not once did I mention feeling guilty. I also didn't mention the judgment I used to pass on myself.

Speaking from past experience, when you work full-time in a corporate setting, there are expectations—from management, from your team, from your subordinates, from your peers—and many of these expectations are passed along from the top down. If the CEO says it's company policy to work from 8:00 AM to 5:00 PM with a one-hour lunch break, then that behavior becomes expected of you. If your boss tells you that checking your personal email should be done on your own time, then not checking Gmail during work hours becomes expected of you. If you watch a coworker get scolded for packing up early, even if it's for a good reason, that signals a certain expectation of you.

For me, I'd been fortunate enough to have a semi-flexible work schedule. *Unfortunately*, I'd reported to a manager who'd had a serious complex about how his employees should spend their work hours. Every single minute of every single day had to be dedicated to something work-related. I know what you might be thinking. *They're paying you to work there, of course you should be doing work-related activities!*

And you're right.

But not to the extent I've experienced.

When I worked full-time, mornings were an absolute nightmare. My boss always showed up at an ungodly hour (I'm talking 5 AM), so by the time I got there around eight o'clock, he was already well into his workday—meaning that I never felt like I could get ahead. I was always playing catch up. He frequently had a list *miles* long for me to attend to, so all of my emails and projects were forced to take a backseat.

"Working lunches" quickly became the new norm. If you've never participated in a working lunch, it basically consists of shoveling food down your throat in a conference room while simultaneously conducting and/or participating in a meeting. This may not sound like a big deal—and if it's once or twice a week, it isn't—but when it becomes a daily thing that you are required to participate in . . . Houston, we have a *serious* problem. It got to a point where I couldn't, for the life of me, recall what having "time alone" at the office even felt like.

Afternoons were always a toss-up. If my boss was stuck on conference calls, then I could finally get all the work done (*my* work) that I'd never even had the chance to start on earlier that day. Even so, he'd still pop his head into my office like a woman on The Bachelor (*Can I steal you for a second?*) and ask for my opinion on this email, that spreadsheet, this presentation . . . you get the idea.

So why am I sharing this story with you? What does all of this have to do with the guilt complex? Well, when I finally *did* quit that job to become a full-time creative entrepreneur, not only was my success 100% dependent on *me*, I also had to redefine what "work" as a whole would look like.

At the time of writing this book, I've been happily self-employed for over a year, and yet my guilt complex *still* trips me up every now and again (first class seats and all).

Believe me, I've done the mindset work around this. I know where my overachievement stems from and I also know that it directly ties into my feeling guilty for "taking breaks" and having "rest days". If I'm not *achieving*, then I'm not *doing*. And if I'm not *doing*, then I'm just *being*. And *being* is lazy . . . except it's **not**.

Guilt is undeniably linked to fear of judgment and/or shame. My entire life—from my childhood all the way through my corporate career—I'd been taught that *not* doing things was shameful. That people who didn't do things were lazy—*those* were the types of people who would never get ahead in life. Talk about an overachiever's worst nightmare!

To combat this? Do, do, do. Keep doing, more and more and more, until you can't possibly fall under the same umbrella as a *lazy* person. Ah, look—the judgment disorder makes yet another unscheduled appearance.

Not surprisingly, my guilt complex hit its peak the entire month after I'd quit my full-time corporate gig. I'd wake up each morning, excited to start my day, but there was always an underlying feeling of guilt. A frequent thought that'd cross my mind was, "So many people are stuck at work right now in a job they hate, so I need to be doing *all* the things I used to wish I could do during the workday, like write at Starbucks, shop at Barnes & Noble at 1:00 in the afternoon, or go for brunch on a random weekday and have a mimosa." It was as if, all of a sudden, I felt guilty for all the things I potentially could be missing out on now that I wasn't constrained by a typical 9-5 job.

For years, all I'd wanted was freedom, but as soon as I got it, I then felt guilty for having it—and guilty if I didn't make the most of it.

Friends, there's so much we can feel guilty for. We can feel guilty for forgetting to call our friends back. Cancelling on brunch at your mother-in-law's. Not ticking off all the boxes on your to-do list. Making a mistake or two. Taking time for yourself.

And then what do we do? We apologize.

*I'm sorry, I'm sorry, I'm sorry.*

Saying sorry means we feel ashamed—like we did something wrong. But is it wrong that you forgot to call a friend back because you were so engrossed in a creative project that time completely got away from you? Is it wrong that you cancelled brunch because you needed a day to recharge in peace and quiet with a good book? Is it wrong that you left half your to-do list undone because you decided to spend quality time playing with your kids in the backyard instead?

Guilt will eat you alive if you let it.

The next time you choose one thing over another, instead of apologizing and saying, "I'm sorry for . . .", I want you to try something else. Instead of "I'm sorry for", say "thank you for".

*I'm sorry I'm late* turns into *Thank you for waiting.*

*I'm sorry I made a mistake* turns into *Thank you for your support and encouragement.*

*I'm sorry I missed brunch* turns into *Thank you for understanding.*

It's such a small thing, this choice of words, but it makes all the difference. At least it has for me.

While the source of guilt may vary from situation to situation, there *is* a common denominator: the "should" factor. And the "should" factor is directly related to our attachment syndrome (hello again) because when we're attached to a certain outcome, concept, or identity, we're immediately drawn into what "should" happen or what we "should" be doing. A hardworking employee *should* stay past regular work hours to finish a project. A selfless mother *should* spend more time with her kids versus spending time alone. A good student *should* turn her homework in on time and get straight As. A dedicated business owner *should* scale their business to new heights, even if it means sacrificing their health and a good night's sleep. These **labels**, and the judgments of these labels, result in "should" behaviors.

You know what you "should" be doing?

Whatever the hell you want. It's **your** life.

Before I quit my full-time job, I'd made the decision that I wanted to spend more of my time volunteering. After weeks of research and deliberation, I finally settled on an organization (which will remain unnamed) that seemed like a good fit at the time.

The initiation process for this organization was quite rigorous. It required more time, effort, and dedication than I care to admit—but I was so excited to volunteer and work with the incredible charities that this particular organization had ties with. In the beginning, things started off great—more than great, really. I was having fun, meeting new people in my community, and truly felt like I was making a difference. But then something entirely unexpected happened.

Guilt.

Things shifted—and not in a good way. Requirements became more stringent, the organizational structure changed, and what once felt like volunteering turned into a bureaucratic race for who could peg more hours, more donors, more *money*. I felt as though I'd been thrust into a political campaign for no one's gain other than the elusive pockets that seemed to sink deeper and deeper.

Sign in. Sign out. Check in. Check out. This many hours for this type of volunteering. That many hours for that type of fundraiser. The guilt would pile up with each box I checked, with each timestamp I wrote on those damn clipboards. Were we volunteering out of the goodness of our hearts, or aiming to "do good" in a way that, in fact, wasn't good for anybody?

Volunteers were disgruntled. Those receiving our help weren't grateful. And all that seemed to matter was how much *money* we could raise. If I'd just wanted to give money, I would have gladly written a check and been on my merry little way. But that's not what I'd signed up for. Giving my *time*—my precious, precious time . . . that's all I'd wanted.

How sad it is to develop guilt around giving. That's exactly what happened to me. I knew what I had to do.

I quit.

I now volunteer on my own time—as an individual, not as part of an organization—and the difference it's made is tenfold. I've been able to get back to the spirit of giving, helping others, being of service . . . all the things that had gotten so twisted when a volunteer organization tried to become something it never should have wanted to be in the first place. The *way* in which I gave my time while in that organization was not aligned with *me*—with who I am as a person. It also wasn't aligned with the person I envisioned myself becoming. So I let it go. And I didn't feel an ounce of guilt in doing so.

In what areas of your life do you feel a sense of guilt?

What "should" story are you playing every day?

Does it *feel* right?

Soulflow dies in the wake of *should*. Should I do this? Should I do that? The *should* doesn't matter because it was designed for, and by, the external. Here's a label, a title, an identity—this is what it looks like and this is what you *should* do if you want to become that.

Some people might think I *should have* stayed in my

corporate job. That I *should have* stayed in Arizona instead of moving to Texas. That I *should have* pursued traditional publishing instead of self-publishing. That I *should* have waited to do this thing or not pursued that thing or blah, blah, blah. That I *should* do something, and then when I decide not to, I *should* feel guilty about it.

How about . . . no? Not now, not today, not ever.

I'm done with *should*. I'm done with *guilt*. If I had listened to all the *shoulds*, where would I be now? It certainly wouldn't be here . . . and here is pretty damn great.

P.S. This first class seat really paid off—that's 2,801 words in the bag!

# Reflection

What *should* stories do you find yourself falling prey to? In what situations, or around what people, do you feel like you *should* act a certain way? What choices have you made in line with *should* and why did you act on those? Was there a time in your past where you made your own choices and were made to feel ashamed?

The next time you feel guilty, take a moment to stop what you're doing (or excuse yourself from a situation) and pinpoint *why* you feel that guilt rising. If there's someone in your life who's constantly making you feel this way, it might be time to have a frank conversation with them. If it's all in your head, then give yourself permission to **not** feel guilty. How will you commit to overcoming your guilt complex? Write down some positive affirmations in the space below. For example, if you struggle with taking time for yourself, your affirmation could be: *I love myself enough to step away and take a break. I deserve to rest.*

_____

_____

_____

_____

_____

_____

_____

_____

_____

_____

_____

_____

_____

_____

_____

_____

_____

_____

_____

_____

_____

# chapter nine

## THE RESISTANCE CRISIS

I CAME ACROSS an inspiring mantra once that said, "I am courageous enough to move *through* the discomfort." It had me so inspired that I dedicated a podcast to that very topic, and it's now led me to write an entire chapter for this book.

I, like many of you, deeply value my relationships and connection with others. I am loyal to a fault. Blame it on my earth sign energy (Taurus and proud!)—but I've found that the one thing I struggle with most is *harmony* in my relationships . . . more specifically, the give and take.

I'm a giver. I know this about myself. I give and give and give until there's nothing left. I'm the person who would be there in a New York minute if a friend or family member needed me. I'm the person who would lend boatloads of cash to someone in need and never expect it to be returned. I'm the person who always goes over the Christmas "spending limit" because the joy I feel when I see my loved ones' faces light up is worth more than the money that is no longer in my bank account. I give so much of my energy—my *heart*—and I never expect anything in return. And not because that might be seen as "selfless"— but because I truly *do not judge* how another person lives their life or chooses to express their appreciation.

Sounds great, doesn't it?

But here's the downfall. I'm taken advantage of often. I'm energetically zapped. I bleed my precious energy into every relationship, except for the one with myself. It's really not surprising that, over time, resentment begins to build. An uncharted level of discomfort surfaces.

And then . . . resistance.

When things change, familiarity fades. Discomfort arises because things are different, new . . . we're not sure exactly how to feel about it, right? So we resist it.

It's a vicious cycle. Change is the only constant and yet our immediate response whenever something changes is to resist it—to put our hand up and say, "No. Not yet. Why is this happening? This isn't the right time."

Simply put, we don't want to be uncomfortable—even though we *know* that in order move forward and plow ahead, we must experience a certain level of discomfort.

So what's with the resistance?

Why do we push back every single time?

Becoming too attached to something, like we talked about previously, is a major part of resistance, but I think there's something much larger at play here.

*Fear.*

The fear that right now—that this current situation—is the best it's *ever* going to get for you. The belief that it can only go downhill from here. Even if you're not crazy-in-love with how things are right now, for some reason, when change sticks its head in your doorway, your first instinct is to cover yourself and shut the door.

To hide and push it out.

When fear takes the wheel, it's almost like we go into survival mode. Our brains begin to rationalize all the reasons why this change is going to be bad. Bad, bad, bad. Any potential for good? Thrown out the window. It doesn't even exist.

*Break up with him? Are you crazy? He only cheated that one time. Better to be with someone than be alone!*

*Pursue a different career path other than one on Wall Street? My parents would never accept it. We're a numbers family. I could never make a living writing and playing my music anyway.*

*Move to a different state? But I've lived here my whole life! What if I hate it? What if I can't figure my life out and have to move back and live with my parents?*

*Quit my job? I hate this job, but they pay me well. I'll never find a job that even comes close to this salary! It's smart to stay a few more years.*

Reading through each one of these makes me want to run around the world and shake people awake. This isn't life! Those thoughts are not based on anything except your perception! When your brain (your ego) tries to rationalize your fears, it also instills a sense of permanence in the choice *it* wants you to make. The *logical* choice—aka the path of least resistance.

When you consider leaving a toxic relationship, your ego tells you that if you don't stick it out, you'll end up alone. Why do we always go to the worst-case scenario? How many people have you dated? If it's more than one, then that's proof right there that your ego's full of shit.

Is it *hard* to break up with someone you care about? Absolutely! There will likely be crying and lonely days and times where you'll doubt yourself—but you know what's worse? Being miserable for the rest of your life. Your ego doesn't show you that part, does it? No, it only highlights what it *wants* you to see—the "comfortable" choice.

The same principle applies for any sort of *change* in our lives, especially when it involves *removing* something. We get used to having something, so when it's about to be "taken away" or (gasp!) we're about to let it go, our ego cranks up the resistance. *What the hell are you thinking? You need that! You won't be able to go on without it!*

Here's the truth. I've broken up with people, and I've been just fine. I've ended friendships, and I've been just fine. I've moved to different states, and I've been just fine. I've quit jobs I've hated, and I've been just fine. I've stopped bending over backwards for people, and I've been just fine.

You. Will. Be. Just. Fine.

It may sound counterintuitive, but in order to thrive—in order to experience *soulflow*—we must embrace discomfort. Embracing discomfort does not mean distracting yourself until the fears and uncertainty go away. It doesn't mean busying yourself with projects and goals to mask what you're really feeling with a false sense of achievement. And it certainly doesn't mean wielding procrastination as a way to play the victim. Embracing discomfort means feeling *all* the feelings. It's not dipping your toe in the water—it's cannonballing into the entire freaking lake in the middle of winter.

We don't know what we don't know. Likewise, we don't feel what we don't feel. If you've never traversed deep into your own emotional abyss, how can you expect your soulflow to surface? How can it possibly exist in such a masked state?

That's all resistance is. A mask. A mask for fear. I'm certainly not proud to say that I've worn that mask throughout many phases of my life, but I have.

I think we all have.

I know I've used my job as an example over and over again in this book, but that's because it's relevant to every chapter I've written. It also just so happens to be the season of life I'm in as I'm drafting this book. So let's use it one more time, shall we? The most I've ever resisted was in quitting a job I despised. Yes, let's reread that.

I resisted *quitting* something that I *hated*.

You see, I'd worked my way up the corporate ladder. From customer service representative to inventory planner to project manager to market segment manager, I experienced many different facets of your "standard" company. Some roles were a better fit than others, but not a single one of them had me gleefully running home to do more work after the day was over.

I knew from the get-go that working for someone else was just a means to an end. An extended interlude. I even had a boss say those exact words to me—and a few months before I decided to quit, he even asked me *why* I wasn't running my business as a coach and author full time. Seems he knew me better than I knew myself.

Ah, but *viva la resistance*. Something in me just wouldn't let me leave. Was it the six-figure salary? No. My business was bringing in more than that. Was it the company car? No. I'd ditched the company car and its hefty number of recalls a few years prior for my own car—one I thought I was worth: a Mercedes-Benz. Was it the health insurance? The 401K? The bonus structure? No. No. No.

I could have quit my job a year earlier than I did. A freaking YEAR. That's how profitable my business was. So why did I stay an entire year past the expiration date? Why did I resist doing something I so clearly wanted?

I'll tell you why. Because working for that company had become my safety net. In my mind, it was stable. Secure. Reliable. I felt that it would be there to catch me if I had a "bad month" in my business.

But for that whole year . . . there were no bad months in my business. Not even when I got sick. Not even when I took the summer off. Instead of embracing the discomfort around the *idea* of quitting, I pushed it away. I told myself that I could find a way to be "comfortable" working two full-time jobs—one I loathed and one I was over-the-moon passionate about.

The thing about safety nets—about security, reliability, and stability—is that they're all just perception. Nothing is inherently stable, secure, or reliable . . . we just perceive them to be that way based on our own experiences, filters, and beliefs.

From a young age, I saw my dad go to work every single morning. I saw what that income provided for our family. I saw his success as he climbed the ranks of each company he worked for. I saw how he was rewarded—the bonuses, the vacations, the luxury cars.

This observation then led me to believe that the only way to achieve financial stability and security was to find a good job—to work for a company and get paid. So to take a risk and go off on my own as an entrepreneur? It's no wonder I resisted! My perception of entrepreneurship equated to that of a rollercoaster ride—risky and full of uncertainty, but also *wildly* appealing.

Was my corporate job truly reliable, stable, and secure? No.

No job is.

In the blink of an eye, management can change, the loss of a huge client can put a company under, or an entire department can be deemed "nonessential" and be dissolved. The resistance I'd felt wasn't so much about quitting . . . it was about what would happen *after* I quit.

The potential consequences.

The disapproval from loved ones.

The judgment from coworkers and complete strangers.

The removal of a steady paycheck.

The realization that my livelihood was *entirely* up to me.

*These* were the things I was resisting. *These* were the things causing me discomfort. They were the unknown—the giant question mark in the middle of my life's journey.

Here's the funny thing about resistance, though. The more you resist something that is *right* for you, the more shit's gonna hit the fan. In the year I stayed at my job (when I should have quit), management changed *three* times, meaning I wasted precious hours giving the same presentations and having the same meetings over and over again; a toxic coworker was added to my team, meaning I was surrounded by drama, gossip, and negativity eight hours a day, five days a week; and a critical member of my team quit, meaning I was left to pick up the slack even though I was already running at 200% capacity.

It got to a point where the discomfort of "the unknown" suddenly looked like freaking *paradise* compared to the dumpster fire I was experiencing every single day at that company. So I quit—but I could have saved myself so much precious time, energy, and brainpower had I just embraced that discomfort . . . had I just *stopped resisting*.

Don't wait for things to become unbearable. Don't allow a situation to continue until you've "hit your breaking point". If something doesn't *feel* right anymore, it's probably because it isn't. And if you're asking for a sign, well . . .

You asking for a sign IS a sign.

That's the only one you'll ever need.

In dealing with discomfort and the inevitable resistance that comes along with it, I now tell myself one thing, and one thing only. *It's this or something better.*

It's this . . . or something better.

So if your "this" ain't lookin' so hot, don't let the discomfort fool you. Don't let resistance hold you back. You have the choice to remove the mask at any time. You hold the power to alter your perception of reality when it is no longer serving you. Let your soulflow be your guiding light because it will lead you right, every single time.

# Reflection

Can you think of a time where you resisted something that ultimately turned out to be for your greater good? Can you recall what worst-case scenario you'd envisioned for yourself during that time? What ended up happening? How did things work out for the better? Write about this experience in the space below with as much detail as possible. Whenever resistance rears its ugly head again, refer back to this page and ask yourself, "What is the *potential* if I stop resisting and just let this take its course?"

_____

_____

_____

_____

_____

_____

_____

_____

_____

_____

_____

_____

_____

_____

_____

_____

# SOULFLOW

# chapter ten

## THE EGO CONSTRUCT

IF YOU'RE FAMILIAR with psychology, then you likely know about "the ego", a term used in a vast range of behavioral studies and theories. If you're not, don't worry—everything we've discussed up until this point is ego-related, meaning that you may already have more of a handle on the concept than you might think.

I saved this particular chapter for later on in the book because it was never my intention to information-dump on psychoanalytic theories in the first few pages. That still isn't my intention. This is a personal development book, not a psychology lesson—and I'm guessing, for those of you who have read my previous books, doing so would have left you wondering who I was and what I'd done with the *real* Kristen. Nevertheless, understanding human personality is key to unlocking awareness of self, so please bear with me as we dip a toe into the dense waters of psychology. By no means am I a psychology expert, which is why I'll be referring to two people who are: Sigmund Freud and Leopold Bellak.

Sigmund Freud is most famous for his psychoanalytic theory of personality, in which he proposes that the personality is composed of three elements—the id, the ego, and the superego. These three elements work together to create complex human behaviors (many of which we've already discussed in previous chapters).

According to Freud's theory, certain aspects of your personality are more primal, meaning they might pressure you to act upon your most basic urges, whereas other parts of your personality work to counteract said urges, thereby aiming to conform to the demands of reality.

Let's start with *the id*. The id is the only component of your personality that is present from birth. This aspect of your personality is entirely unconscious and includes your instinctive and primitive behaviors, which makes it the primary component of your personality. Driven by the *pleasure principle*, it strives for immediate gratification of your desires, wants, and needs—and if not satisfied immediately, can result in anxiety and/or depression.

If this is confusing, think about an infant. When an infant is hungry or uncomfortable, they cry until their needs are satisfied. The id is very important early on in life because it ensures that, as a youngster, your needs are met; however, as we develop, immediately fulfilling our needs is not always realistic or even possible. If the pleasure principle were to run our lives, we'd likely be living in excess, taking things that don't belong to us, and acting in a way that is detrimental to not only our health and safety, but also to those around us.

Next is *the ego*. The ego is the component of your personality that is responsible for dealing with reality. The ego develops **from** the id and ensures that the impulses of the id can be expressed in a way that aligns with that of the real world. It aims to satisfy the id's desires in realistic and socially appropriate ways by weighing the costs and benefits of an action before deciding whether or not to act on it. Since it operates on the *reality principle*, many of the id's urges can be satisfied through a process of delayed gratification, which means that the ego will eventually allow the behavior, but only in the appropriate time and place.

Freud compares the id to a horse and the ego to the horse's rider. The horse provides the power and motion, while the rider provides direction and guidance. Without its rider, the horse may simply wander off and do whatever it so pleases.

Finally we have *the superego*. The superego is the last component of your personality to develop (according to

Freud, it begins to emerge around the age of five). It holds all of our internalized moral standards and ideals that we acquire from the external—like our parents and society (sound familiar?). The role of the superego is to provide guidelines for making judgments.

There are two parts to the superego: 1) **the ego ideal**, which includes the rules and standards for good behavior where obedience of these rules leads to pride, value, and accomplishment; and 2) **the conscience**, which includes things that are viewed as "bad" by society where those behaviors lead to consequences, punishment, guilt, and remorse. The superego is the part of our personality that aims to refine and civilize our behavior by suppressing all unacceptable urges of the id while also struggling to make the ego act upon idealistic standards rather than realistic ones.

The key to a healthy personality, then, would be a balance between the id, the ego, and the superego. When out of balance, Freud believes a maladaptive personality can develop. For instance . . .

An individual with an overly dominant id might become impulsive, uncontrollable, or possibly even criminal since they'd act on their most basic urges without any concern as to whether or not the behavior is appropriate, acceptable, or legal.

Someone with an overly dominant ego might be so tied to reality, rules, and acceptance that they are unable to engage in any type of spontaneous or unexpected behavior (ahem, fear). They become rigid, incapable of accepting change, and might even lack an internal sense of right and wrong.

An overly dominant superego might lead to a personality that is extremely moralistic and judgmental, one that is unable to accept anything or anyone that it perceives as "bad" or "immoral".

Can we see how this might be a problem? If left unchecked, any one of these can result in discord in some aspect of our lives—the pretty important aspects, if I do say so myself: your basic urges, your moral values, and your perception of the world around you.

According to Leopold Bellak, an expert on psychological tests, there are twelve major functions of "the ego", which include reality testing; judgment; sense of reality of the world and the self; modulating and controlling drives, affects, and impulses; object or interpersonal relations; thought processes; defensive functioning; autonomous functioning; adaptive regression in the service of the ego; stimulus barrier; mastery-competence; and synthetic-integrative function. We could go through each one of these, but then this would most definitely turn into a psychology lesson, and I already promised I wouldn't do that. So we'll only focus on one of these (defensive functioning) in a later chapter.

As far as *this* chapter goes, though, there's a reason I titled it *The Ego Construct*. The desired outcome of "the ego construct" isn't necessarily to rid yourself of your ego entirely—it's more along the lines of becoming *aware* that it even exists in the first place, and, furthermore, to construct the narrative in a way that feels balanced, aligned, and authentic *to you*.

Once we become aware of our impulses, our triggers, our habits, and our thought patterns, we can then assess whether or not these things are attributing to our highest good. If they're not, then it's time to construct a new narrative.

The easiest way I've found to "check" my ego is to be the gentle observer of my thoughts. Without judgment, I observe my thoughts as they flow through my mind and traverse layer after layer of consciousness, but I always bring each thought to a grinding halt before it can turn into an action, or worse, a permanent **resident**.

Your mind is precious real estate—just like a landlord, make sure you're charging rent for each thought that takes up space. If the thought doesn't "pay on time" (serve you in a positive way), behaves like a disgruntled tenant would (causes anxiety or stress), or threatens your livelihood in any way, shape, or form, it's time to boot that thought and clear the space, hence opening up "room" for a better, more aligned thought.

The point I'm trying to make is that we should "interview" each thought as if it *were* a potential tenant. It doesn't have to be a long interview—one or two questions will suffice like . . .

*Is this thought fact, or is it merely perception?*

*Is there, perhaps, another way of looking at this and, if so, what does that new way look like?*

By assessing each thought individually, we don't give it the chance to snowball into an entire fear-blizzard that buries everything in its wake. We bring our thoughts to the forefront, question their validity, then decide whether or not it can stay or if it needs to go.

It's really that simple . . . and that difficult.

In consciously constructing the narrative around your ego, you're essentially creating your reality. When you shift your thoughts, perceptions, and feelings, you simultaneously shift your external reality.

Throughout this process, you may find that certain things that used to bother you . . . really don't have much of a hold on you anymore. That conflict, both internally and externally, ceases. That life is simple and clear instead of being muddied with pressure, expectations, and judgment.

You have the power to construct and deconstruct your reality, over and over again, as many times as you need until you find the one that sticks.

If that isn't empowering . . . well, I don't know what is.

# Reflection

For one week, make it a point to keep a notepad and pen with you (or use the Notes app on your phone). I'm not going to ask you to track every single thought (because we have over 60,000 a day so that would be impossible), but to take note of the thoughts that seem to repeat themselves, especially if they're negative or limiting. Document any and all phrases starting with *"I wish"* or *"I can't"* or *"I should"*. Doing this will increase your awareness around these thoughts.

After the week is over, return to this page and work through each of those thoughts. Ask the two questions posed in this chapter: *Is this thought fact, or is it merely perception?* and *Is there, perhaps, another way of looking at this and, if so, what does that new way look like?*

Make sure you review these new stories you've written often. Pretty soon, those limiting thoughts will fade because you've written new and better thoughts to take their place.

_____

_____

_____

_____

_____

_____

_____

# SOULFLOW

# chapter eleven

## THE DIVINE FEMININE

I'VE BEEN TRYING to figure out exactly how I want to begin this particular chapter and it only feels natural to do what I've been doing all along.

To paint a picture by telling a story.

So that's exactly what I'll do.

But in order for it to make sense, it's important that you know something first—something about my morning routine. I start off every single morning by pulling a few Tarot cards for a reading (in case you're wondering, I own *The Wild Unknown* Tarot and Animal Spirit Decks by Kim Krans). The Animal Spirit card I drew this particular morning stirred something deep within me—and took me to a level of awareness I didn't even know I had.

I want to share that with you.

Before pulling that Tarot card, I'd woken up, put my slippers on, and headed for the bathroom. I'd splashed some cold water on my face, brushed my teeth, and was about to put my contact lenses in—but something that morning was different . . . *good* different.

As I stood just inches from the mirror, contact lens balancing on my fingertip, I saw something—in my eyes.

It was just a flash but it was there.

And it certainly wasn't my ego.

For the first time in a long time, I paused. I took in the size of my pupils, the dots of gold and hazel in an otherwise greenish-grey landscape. I sensed the calmness and tranquility that comes with starting a new day, *before* we become unhinged by responsibilities, to-do lists, and impossibly high expectations. I saw worth and love and tenderness. I saw *Her*—the Divine Feminine.

I saw *me*.

And then, just like that, She was gone.

Befuddled (I love this word and I hardly every get to use it), I'd wandered into the kitchen, brewed myself a cup of tea, then carried my Tarot deck onto the patio and began to shuffle the cards. The Animal Spirit card that fell onto my lap rendered me speechless. It was **The Dragon**:

*"When we look in the mirror, we may glimpse the 'self behind the self', the one who is always watching us . . . guiding us."*

**The self behind the self.**

For the first time in thirty years, I saw Her. It dawned on me that while that contact lens helps me *see* in a literal sense, it couldn't help me *see* on a soul level. How often do we look in the mirror without actually *looking*, without actually *seeing*? Do we ever truly *see* ourselves?

*All* of ourselves?

I'd like to believe that every single one of us holds the potential to reach full awareness of Self—but I'm not so sure it's a place we can arrive at. Someday, maybe. Perhaps when our souls are no longer attached to this Earthly realm. Full awareness of Self is more of a journey—our *soulflow* journey.

You see, this glimpse of the Divine Feminine caught me off guard because the masculine has been at play for most of my life. Masculine energy—the *doing*, the *action*, the *achieving*—is what I've known best. As you well know after reading previous chapters, it's what I've identified with. My twenties were heavily focused in this arena . . . on how much I could *do*. In one of my favorite books, *Lunar Abundance*, author Ezzie Spencer mentions how this shift in mindset can happen at an early age. It's actually quite simple . . . and quite tragic.

Throughout girlhood, I identified with my father. No surprise here, but he exuded masculine energy. As a young girl looking up to him, I then immersed myself in that energy. I absorbed it. I made it my own. That was a defining moment for me. Without even realizing it, I'd accepted the masculine and rejected the feminine.

I certainly don't regret how my childhood happened to unfold, or how my life has played out up to this point. I acknowledge that my life would look very, *very* different without the influence of masculine energy—but I am now overtly aware that I had forsaken one for the other. I shoved my feminine energy so far down for so many years that it couldn't possibly resurface . . . and what's worse is that I didn't *want* it to come up for air because I knew exactly what would happen once it did.

I would *feel*.

And I'm not just talking about surface level emotions, like feeling happy or sad or angry. I'm talking about something much greater—the feelings that reverberate deep within your core. It's hard to explain what this feels like because I imagine it's different for everyone.

This afternoon, I was swinging in my hammock in the backyard, watching the hawks soar in the breeze and the leaves rustle in the trees. I closed my eyes as the sun emerged from behind a cloud, a sudden fiery heat radiating throughout my entire body. It was so powerful that I could feel it against the backs of my eyelids.

Instinctively, my eyes began to water.

With tears streaming down my face, I smiled—not for any particular reason, but because I *felt* like it. I felt overjoyed, grateful, and blessed to be in that moment—a moment where I could feel the heat and the breeze and the gentle sway of the hammock, working in tandem with gravity. I've experienced so many more moments like this now that I've welcomed feminine energy back into the picture.

As someone who hardly used to express emotions, crying in the middle of the day—simply because I feel like it—is a pretty big shift. Allowing myself to *feel* has been one of the greatest gifts I've ever given myself. I am thirty years old at the time of writing this, and I am just now acclimating to this feminine energy. Maybe "acclimate" is the wrong word; perhaps I'm becoming *reacquainted* with it—and it's beautiful.

The Divine Feminine does not try to be something She's not. She doesn't judge or compare, worry or fear. She is quiet, yet deliberate. Peaceful, yet resolute. Not always seen or heard, but significant beyond measure. She's behind every thought, every decision, every action, every feeling. She guides without pushing.

She requires **nothing** yet gives *everything*.

Getting to know this feminine energy has been one of the greatest joys of my life. In a way, it feels like a return home—something that's impossible to explain in words because, again, it's a *feeling*. Like when you pull into the driveway of your family home for the first time in five years. Or the way your mom always smells of bergamot and patchouli when she wraps you in her embrace. The way your sister lights up when she flings open the door to greet you. The way your dad looks at you, every single time . . .

like you're still his little girl—and always will be.

That feeling of *home*.

That's what the Divine Feminine feels like for me . . . except it's wrapping myself in my own loving embrace. It's feeling the corners of my eyes crinkle as a sincere smile spreads across my face. It's catching myself in the mirror— my *true* Self—with steadfast conviction that I am worthy, deserving, and loved no matter what.

No. Matter. What.

This isn't to discredit the masculine. Masculine energy has taught me so much about my thoughts, behaviors, and actions. It's helped me create a life that I am beyond proud of. In no way has one replaced the other—I've just become self-aware. Aware that, for me, my *doing* falls under the masculine and my *being* falls under the feminine.

That my *doing* is more susceptible to fear, whereas my *being* is grounded in love.

One of these energies might stick out to you like a sore thumb. Some of you might know exactly which one has been at play for most of your life. For others, the answer might not be so obvious. Between *being* and *doing*, ask yourself where you feel most comfortable.

Do you enjoy waking up and making mile-long to-do lists, knowing that you get to tackle the day? If so, you may be more prone to masculine energy. If the thought of a to-do list makes you cringe and you'd rather just float through the day, the scales might be tipped more toward the feminine. Embracing both is a delicate balance, one where you hope to *do* without your ego getting in your head, and one where you hope to *be* without your id telling you it needs this or that *now, now, now*.

It's in the Divine Feminine, in this state of *being*, that we can rest, release, and surrender while also opening up space to draw inspiration. It's in the masculine that we can take that space and inspiration to serve and create in line with our soul purpose. That soul purpose—and our soulflow— are intrinsically linked to the delicate balance of these energies.

I say this all the time, but I'll say it again. Too much of one thing is never a good thing. Constant striving can lead to burnout. Inaction can lead to undesirable vices. It's in the balance, in the yin and the yang, that we can finally begin to understand just what our soulflow has been trying to reveal to us all along . . .

That we are enough, right now, as we are.

## Reflection

Do you identify more with masculine energy (action and doing) or the feminine (emotion and being)? What role does each play in your life? Is there one you'd like to incorporate more of? If so, how will you commit to doing this? If you want to embrace the masculine, perhaps you'll finally initiate that long awaited project, or speak your mind in the next meeting at work, or try something new, even if it scares the living daylights out of you. If you want to embrace the feminine, perhaps you'll create space in your day for feeling and being. Perhaps you'll meditate with crystals and essential oils. Perhaps you'll watch a movie that gives you all the feels and makes you cry. Perhaps you'll perform a cleansing ritual to remove unwelcome energy (like saging your house). What will you *do*? How will you *be*?

_____

_____

_____

_____

_____

_____

_____

_____

_____

_____

_____

_____

_____

_____

_____

_____

_____

_____

_____

# chapter twelve

## THE FEAR RELEASE

WOULD IT SURPRISE you to learn that every time I open my laptop, with my fingers splayed across the keyboard, I feel a tinge of fear? It's not an overwhelming sense of fear. There are no crashing waves of self-doubt. There's no crippling anxiety. There's no repetition involving thoughts of *I can't, I can't, I can't.*

It's just a *dash* of fear. Nothing more. Like when a recipe calls for a pinch of salt. It's between my thumb and index finger one minute, sitting in a mixing bowl the next.

This is the ninth book I've written (the seventh that'll be published), yet every time I sit down to write, that trace of fear emerges. It's almost as if its appearance is for the sole purpose of warning me, "*Hey, are you sure you want to do this? Put another piece of your soul out into the world?*"

My answer is always yes—and it's always yes because I know that that's just my ego talking.

Everything you've read up until this point has focused largely on fear and the many different masks it wears when it's trying to keep us comfortable . . . to keep us "safe". While we can't get rid of fear altogether, we *can* influence the impact it has on our day-to-day lives.

Fear is nothing more than our belief in our own ego-run imaginations. What do I mean by this? Seeing as we now understand how the id, the ego, and the superego work together to affect our personality, we can then come to the conclusion that our entire reality is a perception that our egos have created—one that's been entirely imagined based on our thoughts, feelings, and reactions with regard to our past experiences.

Releasing fear requires removal, and while we can't exactly remove the ego, we *can* remove the belief in it.

Let's use my earlier example of fear cropping up whenever I sit down to write. Whether you have trace amounts of fear or tend to feel completely paralyzed by its presence will largely depend on *how strong* your belief is in your ego's version of reality. Here are some thoughts that pop up when my fear of writing a book emerges:

*I doubt anyone's even going to read this. But if they do . . .*
*What if they hate it? What if they say terrible things?*

*What if even more people agree with them?*
*Maybe I've made too many mistakes to be writing a book.*
*What if I fail? What if I can't finish writing it?*
*Maybe I'm not good enough to do this.*

Do we see the giant fear-blizzard that's forming? How one fear-based thought snowballs into an even bigger one? The first thought, while not completely self-deprecating, is the one that sets everything in motion. It's usually quiet, one that you'll say almost jokingly to yourself, but it's also the one that opens the door, inviting the more harmful thoughts in.

Ergo, it's the most dangerous.

Have you ever heard the quote, "Doubt kills more dreams than failure ever will"? There's a reason it's said over and over again.

It's because **doubt** is the silent killer of dreams.

Doubt is the catalyst for fear. The moment you listen to doubt, even if it's just a flash, is the same moment you've accepted your ego's version of reality as the truth.

The trick is to catch your doubt *before* it has an opportunity to walk through the doors of your mind and invite the rest of its friends in. Catching doubt "in the action" is a lot like waiting for water to boil. Say you fill up a teakettle with water and put it on a hot stove. You may sit there and wait, or you may decide to leave it unattended for a bit—but you *know*, at some point, that that kettle is going to start whistling. When it does, what's the first thing you do?

You rush over to it and take if off of the stove.

You *remove it* from **the source**.

Likewise, you can separate your doubt from your ego.

Just like hot water, doubt simmers and simmers below the surface, waiting until you're not looking, and then WHAM! Suddenly, you're surrounded by nonstop high-pitched shrieking—except it's inside your brain instead of in the kitchen. What happens if you don't remove the kettle from the heat, from its source?

It gets louder and **louder**. And it won't stop . . .

Until you *remove* it.

By the same logic, when a doubtful thought enters your mind, instead of letting it shriek (and give way to even more fear-based thoughts), move it *away* from the heat source (in this case, your ego). Moving doubt *away* from your ego exposes the source. Suddenly, your ego has nowhere to hide. It can't hurl additional fear-based thoughts at you because you're *aware* of its presence.

You're aware of what it's *trying* to do.

It may try to put up a fight, but that's the exact moment you can shut it down for good. And you can do that by saying, "I hear you, but I choose my truth. And my truth is, and always will be, **love**."

Return to love every single time . . . because love does not doubt, fear, or worry. It does not limit, restrict, or take. It gives. It nourishes. It ignites.

It is *the* unconditional Source.

Pretty hard to fight with that, if I do say so myself.

When our lives are shadowed by doubt and fear, that's exactly what we're bound to do—live in the shadows. We'll keep repeating the same patterns, picking the same fights (with ourselves and with other people), feeling guilty over the same things . . . until we finally **own our truth**.

And by *own it*, I mean fully believe in it.

Fear is tricky in that it makes you *think* you're getting what you need when, in reality, it's preventing you from having all the things you truly want. Most people don't leave jobs they hate because fear tells them they're getting what they *need*—a reliable source of income, security, and stability. Many people stay in toxic relationships because fear tells them they *need* to be with someone—it has them believe that the alternative, which is being alone, is a bad thing . . . and permanent. A lot of people face health issues later in life because fear tells them they *need* comfort more than the energy to move their bodies and prepare healthy meals—it's *so* much easier to just order pizza and Netflix-and-chill.

Your ego tells you that you *need* these things, even if they're not the right fit anymore (or never were) or you've outgrown them. It tells you that you *need* them because they're safe. Familiar. Comfortable. To want **more** than what you *need*? Well that's just selfish.

Except it isn't.

Your ego is desperate for you to believe in its perceived reality—the one you *need*, which is hardly ever in line with the one you actually *want*. It won't lay out the consequences of staying comfortable because it *knows* that once you get a look at the other side—at what you really want and how much is indeed possible—you'll be running for the hills, arms flailing, screaming, "Yes! I surrender to the possibility of LIFE!"

And guess what? Once you start running, you'll keep running. Your fear will have no choice but to melt away because it won't be able to catch up to you. Your ego will quickly realize that it no longer has control, but even so, it'll try to rein you in with all of its old tricks and schemes— with consumption, judgment, rejection, attachment, resistance, guilt—but once you're aware, you are **aware**. And there is no taking that away from you.

In one of my favorite books by Shannon Kaiser, *Adventures For Your Soul*, she lays out the ten most common fears, which include:

1. Fear of failure
2. Fear of the unknown
3. Fear of not having enough
4. Fear of change
5. Fear of shame or judgment
6. Fear of intimacy, loss of self, or loss of freedom
7. Fear of being alone
8. Fear of rejection
9. Fear of losing love (dying or losing loved ones)

10. Fear of inadequacy

We've discussed many of these fears throughout this book, as well as where they stem from and how they play out over time if they go unmanaged. Lack of acceptance results in fear of failure, fear of rejection, fear of shame or judgment, fear of intimacy, and fear of inadequacy. Lack of control results in fear of the unknown, fear of not having enough, fear of change, fear of being alone, and fear of losing love. What do the need for acceptance and control always circle back to?

Your worth.

Self-love.

Unless you make a conscious effort to stop it, your ego will continue to show you all the ways in which you are unworthy. It'll show you all the ways in which it's tried to keep you "safe":

*You failed that English test in fourth grade, so you're safe working as a clerk at this department store because no judgment on writing takes place here. Even safer, there's no writing or creative expression at all!*

*Your move to California won't work out because your last move didn't either. Stay here where it's safe. You have everything you could ever need. Why would you want to give that up?*

*Pursue being a musician? Are you insane? You're too old, have no connections, and you certainly don't have the money to buy a guitar. Why go after music when practicing law is a sure thing?*

The success of your ego relies on two things: the

happenings of the past and the unknowns of the future. It uses your past experiences—ones that didn't go so well—to try and scare you out of taking risks; but it also uses the uncertainty of the future to keep you playing small. It rarely focuses on the present, on the *actual* reality.

Your *true* reality.

All you need to know is this. If there's a glimmer of hope and light—something that keeps showing up in your awareness, something that makes you feel like *you*, even if it's just for a brief moment—**that's** something worth paying attention to. The whisperings of your heart, however faint, are from your soul. It's your soul purpose waiting for you to close the door on fear and open up the one it's been standing behind for years and years . . . probably since you were a child. If something keeps showing up, it is *worth* pursuing.

Your soulflow is worth pursuing.

**You** are worth pursuing.

So open the door.

## Reflection

I'm going to be blunt. The process of releasing your fears isn't going to be a walk in the park. It's likely going to dredge up a lot of unresolved feelings—pain, guilt, insecurity, anger, remorse. This is just your ego retreating further into the onion as you peel it away, layer by layer.

Like a toddler, your ego may lash out at you. It may attempt to give you the silent treatment. It may run away from you to go hide in the closet. I encourage you to respond to your ego the same way you would a child—with compassion, sincerity, and love. Our egos are the parts of us that have been hurting for a long, *long* time. They'd rather stay hidden than face discomfort—but in order to move past our fears, we must bring them out into the open. We must give our fears space to breathe without resistance, judgment, or guilt.

Of the ten fears listed in this chapter, which ones do you resonate with most? Which ones keep you up at night? Which ones seem to pop up whenever you're about to make a big decision? Make note of them below.

Then review whether the source of that fear comes from lack of acceptance or lack of control. Recall what situation(s) from your childhood first made you feel rejected or out of control. And then . . . vow to release it.

Surrender. Forgive. *Let go.* If you need to, cry it out. If you need to scream into a pillow, then do that. If you need to break some plates, you can do that, too. Light a fire and burn whatever needs to be burned. Call whoever may have had a part in introducing these fears to you for no other reason than to tell them that you love them.

Fear can only have its hooks in you if you *think* it does. It's time to release it. It's time to let fear go.

# SOULFLOW

# chapter thirteen

## THE DISTRACTION OVERHAUL

AS MUCH AS I wish tapping into your soulflow was as easy as just releasing your fears, that's only half of the equation. The other half is much more discreet—and frankly, a bit more intimidating.

It's what I like to call the distraction overhaul.

Whether we're aware of them or not, we all have defense mechanisms that can pop up even *after* we've released our fears. It's the ego's one last retaliation. It's Plan B, since Plan A (fear mongering) didn't quite work out. It's the literal safety net—to keep you playing safe.

The first thing you might think of when you hear the term *defense mechanism* is the way in which we respond to negativity. If someone points out one of our flaws, a defense mechanism might be to attack back by pointing out one of *their* flaws. If someone says they don't understand something we've said or done, we might overcompensate for our own lack of self-acceptance by over-explaining or trying to "justify" our behavior.

The defense mechanisms of the ego are similar. It's aware that you've acknowledged your fears and that you've released them—but that doesn't mean it still can't try to derail you from going after what you really want. It just knows it can't play the "fear card" anymore.

So what can it play? Well, while you're on offense, it's going to play defense—in this case, defense falls under the umbrella of *distraction* . . . like procrastination. Or indecision. Or micromanaging.

Your ego is the **master** of distraction.

When you acknowledge and release your fears, suddenly there's more *space*. We'd be wise to fill that space with our *soulflow*—with dreams, plans, and inspired action—but, don't forget, your ego still wants to keep you safe. And as far as *it's* concerned, any plans or action related to your soulflow **aren't** safe. So, instead of filling that space with all the things that can get you closer to your soulflow, it's going to attempt to fill every inch of that space with *distractions*.

Let's take today, for example. My ego's "distraction attempt" at procrastination got the better of me. I woke up pretty early, fully intending to go through my morning routine and write this chapter. Guess what time it is?

7:15 P.M. . . . and I'm just now writing it.

What's interesting is that I didn't feel any doubt, fear, or uncertainty when I woke up this morning. In fact, I felt confident, recharged, and ready to take on the day. So what happened?

As I was journaling out my intentions for the day, a thought popped into my head (like they so often do). I had forgotten to put some bills in the mailbox the day prior. Mid-sentence, I closed my journal, walked to my office to retrieve the bills, and secured them in the mailbox. As I was making my way back to the front door, I noticed the developing storm clouds overhead. I also noticed the length of my front lawn. *I'll just do this one thing and then be done* . . . **says no one ever**.

So I mowed the lawn. And then proceeded to clean the house. Which then led to decluttering the files in my office. Which then had me sorting through the recycling bin. Which then snowballed into something else that was most definitely *not* writing this chapter.

Simply put, if *we* don't prioritize our time, our egos will do it for us. It'll find something more important, more urgent, more *comfortable* for us to do instead of the things that are actually important to us.

Did mowing the lawn get me one step closer in fulfilling my soul purpose? No. Did cleaning the entire house? Decluttering my office? Sorting through the recycling? No.

No. No.

But writing this chapter? Yes. Very much so.

Now, this isn't to say that mowing and cleaning and decluttering are bad things. On the contrary, they're quite useful in providing the ol' noggin with a clear headspace. The problem is when the ego's distractions *overhaul* your priorities for the entire day. Usually, when I start on a "cleaning spree", I can't stop. Mowing the front lawn turns into also mowing the backyard and cleaning out the garage and clearing out the gutters and watering the garden and realizing the garden needs more plants and then going to Home Depot to buy more plants and soil and then coming home to plant them until . . .

*Hello, dinnertime.*

My ego knows that cleaning is something I'll take to an extreme, so it uses this distraction often to keep me from working on my books and growing my business. This is exactly why I make a **Top 3 List** every single morning.

I write down my three non-negotiables for that day— things I absolutely *must* get done. Sometimes it's a heavier list, like film this YouTube video, record that podcast episode, write two chapters of this project; other days it's a little lighter, like go for a one-mile walk without my phone, read a chapter of a personal development book, answer ten emails. No matter what, though, the items on my Top 3 are always *specific*—and there's always a defined outcome. Filming videos and recording podcast episodes means that there's content for the next week. Writing two chapters of a project means I'm 6,000 words closer to completing the manuscript. Going for a walk without my phone means that I'm disconnected for a bit to reset and recharge. Reading a chapter of a personal development book means I'm fueling my brain and setting myself up for growth. Answering ten emails means I'm staying on top of my business and am open to opportunities.

The ego's distractions *thrive* in **ambiguity**.

Just like it'll *prioritize* for you, if you don't know exactly **how** you're going to spend your time, your ego will *specify* that for you, too.

Prioritization. Specificity. Immediate action.

So, you've made your Top 3 List, you've specified each one with its desirable outcome, and that's all well and good, but now you actually have to **act** on it.

If immediate action isn't possible because of other commitments (like dropping the kids off at school or commuting to work), then set a deadline. Will your Top 3 be done before noon, before you sit down to eat lunch? Or will they be done after dinner, once you've started to wind down and de-stress from the day? Setting a deadline shows that these things truly *are* priorities—that they **matter**.

The great thing about this method is that it works for all types of distractions. Procrastination certainly. But what about indecision? Or shiny new idea syndrome? Or micromanaging? Or scrolling social media?

Let's tackle the first one. Indecision occurs when

overwhelm is present. Usually, when it comes to a project or task, indecision simply means that the project or task in question is *too big*. To reduce overwhelm, try breaking it down into smaller, more actionable items.

For example, if you feel indecisive when it comes to a certain task, like writing a chapter of a book, perhaps that's because first, you need to review your outline. Breaking it down to "review chapter one of outline" or "write one paragraph" or "write one page" is a lot more manageable than diving in and writing the *whole* chapter.

If you feel indecisive when it comes to a big project, like *implement a minimalist lifestyle*, that's probably because the thought of decluttering and getting rid of half your stuff feels comparable to climbing Mt. Everest in the middle of winter. Perhaps smaller tasks, like "sort through handbag collection" or "clean out jewelry drawer", would be less daunting.

Give your mind something **specific** to focus on.

Same goes for shiny new idea syndrome. If an idea for another project comes your way, by all means, write it down! You can capture it while it's fresh in your mind, but that doesn't necessarily mean you have to go full steam ahead and forego the other projects you've been working on up until this point—projects that *still* deserve your energy, focus, and undivided attention. If you find that you're struggling to continue working on current projects, remind yourself of your **why**—why did you start that original project? Write down all the reasons that come to mind.

Again, specificity is key.

Micromanaging, also known as interference, is another type of distraction from your ego. Micromanaging stems from the need for control and not trusting anyone else to "do things right". Setting an intention for the day and specifying what's most important can help put things into perspective. You can't do everything, and even if you *could*, you probably wouldn't do it very well. By loosening the reins and making space for assistance, you're able to suppress your ego's distractions. Why would you do something you've already deemed as nonessential? The distraction of micromanaging has no choice but to take a backseat.

As you well know, scrolling social media, binge-watching Netflix, or going down the YouTube rabbit hole are all forms of consumption. Consumption is one of your ego's favorite distraction tactics because it requires hardly any "doing" on its part. It assures you that there are so many *other* ways to fill your time—watch movies, listen to the news, scroll through Facebook, see what's trending on Twitter, create a new board on Pinterest—not to mention, these things are *so* easily accessible.

We already went through an entire chapter on consumption, so if you need a refresher, feel free to revisit chapter four. There's no denying that consumption satiates our desire for entertainment. Like you, I love plopping onto my couch with a good book, or finally watching the new season of my favorite show, or listening to the most recent episodes of my go-to podcasts. But consumption in moderation is key. Know the difference between "taking a break" and "shutting off for a few" versus consumption as distraction—because it's the easiest form of distraction to fall into . . . and also the hardest to pull yourself out of.

## Reflection

What do you tend to get distracted by the most? The next time you feel a distraction coming on when you have a project or task you want to complete, refer back to this chapter. Make your Top 3 List. Prioritize it. Specify the deadline. Take action.

If distractions keep knocking at your door, review what's truly keeping you from that project or task. Is it, perhaps, too big? Do you feel indecisive about the next steps? Are you worried it'll be too hard? Remember, this is just your ego trying to rope you back into fear. You've already released your fears, so now it's time to overhaul the distractions by taking ownership of how you spend your time. If you own it, your ego can't. Plain and simple.

_____

_____

_____

_____

# chapter fourteen

## THE GRACE MENTALITY

THIS PAST WEEKEND, I didn't touch my computer or phone. Not to toot my own horn, but this is a pretty big deal for someone whose business lives and thrives in the online space. And even when I'm not behind a camera for YouTube or setting up a flatlay for Instagram or answering client emails, I'm still behind a computer, writing the pages for my next book.

But not this past weekend. Just like I've needed fear detoxes in the past, I was in desperate need of a technological detox. So that's exactly what I did.

I shoved my iPhone and Apple watch in the drawer of my nightstand. I logged off both my laptop and my desktop computer. I shut the doors to my office. I hid the remotes to the TV so that they were out of sight. *And then I began my weekend.*

And you know what? Something incredible happened.

Not once did I feel that nagging sense of guilt from my undone to-do list. Not once did I feel the need to consume. Not once did a judgmental thought cross my mind.

It felt like Bali all over again.

Just me and the Universe, in total harmony.

You might be wondering what I did for two whole days without technology. The real question is . . . what *didn't* I do? I enjoyed slow mornings on my back patio with a cup of coffee. I meditated for longer than I ever have before, without even realizing it. I took my dog, Denali, for two walks on each of those days. I read two books, cover to cover. I tended to my garden, planting new herbs and flowers in my backyard. I transformed what used to be my breakfast nook into a very zen greenhouse-like space. I breathed life back into creative projects around the house that I hadn't touched in months.

In a nutshell, I tapped into my *soulflow*.

And it was all because of my **grace mentality**.

Grace is such a beautiful word, isn't it? In looking up the definition, I wasn't surprised to read that, as a noun, it means *simple elegance*. But what I was even more captivated by was the definition of grace as a verb: to do honor or credit to (someone or something) by one's presence. In other words . . . to do honor **to oneself** by *one's presence*.

Doesn't that just make your heart sing?

I can honestly say that this was my most graceful weekend yet. I wasn't in a hurry. I wasn't pressured. I wasn't climbing up the never-ending mountain of *more*.

I took a pause. A long, much-desired pause.

I actually *felt* the damp soil as it slid between my fingers as I tended to my garden. I inhaled the sweet scent of a nearby rose bush as it started to bloom. I befriended a family of ducks on my walk and ran inside to find bread to feed them. I took my time curating a dinner recipe using only what I had in my pantry. I swung outside in my hammock for hours, reading without an end point . . .

Without an expected outcome.

I think that's what grace is, for me at least: doing and being without having an outcome in mind. It's gladly and openly surrendering to the *now*, to this moment that will only happen once in your life.

To do honor *to yourself* by **your own presence**.

What a world this would be if we all showed ourselves a little grace. What a ripple effect it would have.

Have you ever been in line at a Starbucks drive-thru where, after pulling up to the window, credit card in hand, they tell you that the person ahead of you has already paid for your drink? Feels good, doesn't it?

That kind of energy is so contagious, it has you wanting to do the same for the car behind you, no matter how big their order is. It's that pay-it-forward mentality and *damn,* is it powerful. I remember asking the barista once how long that particular Friday's pay-it-forward had been going on for, and he said since five o'clock that morning. It was 8:30 when I'd pulled up. That's over *three hours*—and I don't doubt for one second that it went on for the rest of the day.

Grace and kindness go hand in hand. When we show ourselves grace and kindness, it ripples outward. Let's say you go out of your way to hold the door for someone. Then that person returns a stranger's shopping cart to the corral. Then that person doesn't honk when someone cuts them off in traffic. Then that person gets home in time to enjoy dinner and tuck their kids into bed before leaving on another weeklong business trip.

All because you held the door open.

The best part is that kindness is **free**. All you have to do is make a conscious decision to brighten someone else's day, no matter the size of the gesture. I've found that the smallest gestures tend to have the biggest impacts. Like holding the door open. Buying someone else's latte. Leaving a few dollar bills in library books and putting them back on the shelves. Complimenting a stranger on their outfit. Cheering the kids on in your neighborhood as they whizz by in a "race" on their bikes.

Doing everything with *love*.

When we show ourselves grace, we don't deprive ourselves of bread at dinner because we're "on a diet". We don't stay up until two o'clock in the morning, frantically working on a project, then proceed to lose an entire night's worth of sleep. We don't freak out and yell at our kids when they accidentally spill the contents of their cereal bowls onto the floor. We don't gossip about another person because of some false rumor going around. We don't expend our energy in a negative way because grace reminds us that our energy is precious.

It is *sacred*.

Why are we so inclined to forget this? Why do we engage in activities that keep our soulflow trapped and buried beneath the surface? Why can't we show ourselves, and others, a bit more grace?

I want you to try something called *The Graceful Three*—to yourself, to loved ones, and to strangers. The next time you look in the mirror, I want you to say three things you love about yourself. The next time you see a family member or friend, I want you to tell them three reasons why you admire them, or three reasons why you're grateful for that relationship. The next time you're out in a public place, I want you to make it a point to compliment three people you've never met. I encourage you to do this every single day for a week and see how it impacts you . . . how it makes you *feel*.

We all seem to be on this quest for happiness—to live a joyful life we're wildly passionate about. What if the key to a better life is as simple as showing up for ourselves with grace, compassion, and kindness? What if the key to a fulfilling life . . . is absolutely free?

Now wouldn't that be somethin'?

## Reflection

How will you commit to showing yourself grace this week? How can you show kindness to others? If you don't know where to start, try *The Grateful Three* exercise mentioned in this chapter. Each day for a week, come back to this page and reflect on how it makes you feel. Challenge yourself to keep at it. Can you keep it going past a week? What about a month? Or two? Or three?

_____

_____

_____

_____

_____

_____

_____

_____

_____

_____

_____

_____

_____

_____

# chapter fifteen

## THE PRARABDHA KARMA

WHEN I TRAVELED to India in 2014, I didn't know what to expect, but I remember feeling especially drawn to the culture, history, and languages, both ancient and present. I distinctly remember reading about a concept called Prarabdha Karma, which, in Hinduism, is part of the karma cycle. According to Hindu spiritual teacher Sivananda Saraswati, there are three kinds of karma, including Sanchita (accumulated works), Prarabdha (fructifying works), and Agami (current works).

Now, I'm not an expert in this area (and certainly don't claim to be), but as I continued to read more about Prarabdha Karma, I came across a meaning that really resonated with me. As author Tosha Silver puts it:

Prarabdha Karma is our own soul's course of study.

I quickly fell in love with this school of thought.

We spend most of our lives wondering what our purpose is. Why we're here. If we're "doing life right".

Some of us may try to gain insight by diving into religious practices, studying as many philosophy books as we can get our hands on, or seeking spiritual guidance from those who have come before us. Others may choose to simply not believe in anything.

And that's okay. Because *my* soul's course of study probably looks a lot different than yours. And *yours* probably looks a lot different than your sister's or your mother's or your father's. And *theirs* probably looks a lot different than their parents' and grandparents' and so on.

Your soul's course of study is **unique** to you.

Put another way, in all the galaxies in an infinite universe, there will never be another you, exactly as you are, living the life you're living, pursuing your soul's unique course of study.

Imagine if each and every one of us took this concept to heart . . . the belief and knowledge that everything you are—everything you want to be—is already inside of you at this very moment. That your intuition is there for a reason. That your heart's whisperings are more than just a fleeting murmur in this pocket of space and time. That the guidance you've been longing for is already hardwired into your very existence—into your *soul*.

The need for surface level consumption would disappear. So would judgment, attachment, guilt, and resistance. Think about it . . .

Why would there be a need to consume if the answers were already inside? Why would there be a need to judge if our souls' courses of study were *meant* to be different? Why would there be a need to attach to an identity if your *soul purpose* was the only thing that truly mattered? Why would there be a need to feel guilty if you're just doing and being all the things you need to do and be to pursue your soul's unique course of study? Why would there be a need to resist a life that is destined to unfold exactly when, how, and why it's meant to?

Divine guidance, universal law, Prarabdha Karma, soul purpose, awakening, transformation . . . our soulflow. It all relies heavily on your level of *awareness*—on your perspective of past experiences, your daily thought processes, how much and how deep you allow yourself to feel, and what specific lens you *decide* to look at life through. It's in this state of awareness, in pursuing your Prarabdha Karma, that you can experience your *soulflow*.

Awareness of Self is hard to put into words because it's a *feeling*. You know when you go to sleep at night and wake up in the morning? The act of waking up is where we switch from unconsciousness to consciousness—to a state of awareness. You're aware that your eyes are open. You're aware that you're breathing. You're aware that you can hear and see and smell and touch.

You're aware that you're *alive*.

That awareness when we wake up is similar to the awareness we want to cultivate in our daily lives—where we're fully conscious of our behaviors, actions, and reactions . . . our thoughts, feelings, and overall sense of what it means to *be* us.

What does it mean to *be* you?

What whisperings are subtle, yet recurring?

How has your intuition been trying to guide you?

Have you been listening?

Are you even aware?

*Become* aware. Cultivate. Practice. Flow. Be.

Bali was the first time I opened myself up to this kind of ethereal connection with *Self*. I didn't expect a specific outcome. I wasn't attached to any "shoulds". I didn't judge myself or my experience. And I certainly didn't resist it. On the contrary, I welcomed it.

With a wide and loving embrace, I let it in.

Awareness of Self is not something we have to go searching for because it's already built into our souls. It may take some serious digging, some exploring beneath the surface, some dusting off and rearranging of your mental file cabinets, but the awareness is already there—your *soulflow* is already there. All you have to decide is just how deep you're willing to go to reclaim it.

## Reflection

How will you choose to live every single day from this point forward? What will you embrace? What will you surrender? How will you commit to inviting your *soulflow*, not as a temporary houseguest, but as a permanent resident of your mind, body, and spirit?

_____

_____

_____

_____

_____

_____

_____

_____

_____

_____

_____

_____

_____

_____

_____

_____

_____

_____

_____

_____

_____

# closing thoughts

## FROM THE AUTHOR

I HAVE A confession to make. This book has been both soul traversing and intrusive, and yet it's been my absolute favorite to write. When I was in the process of writing my first personal development book, *Be Your Own #Goals*, I felt . . . different. Not the way I do right now—which is hard to explain since I'm not even really sure what those feelings entail.

Writing this particular book cracked me open in a way no other book has. Perhaps that's because my first book was so outwardly focused—on achievement and going after the life you want with just a smidge of *soulflow* sprinkled in there. That book was initiated like any of my other projects—with deadlines and word count targets and stress and . . . force. As you probably (hopefully) know by now, force is the opposite of flow.

I remember waking up in the mornings, looking at my calendar and my to-do list for the day, opening up my laptop, and reviewing my outline for *Be Your Own #Goals*. I'd cross things out, move things around, reread old sections, and brainstorm entirely new ones. And even when I didn't *feel* like writing, I forced myself to.

However with this book . . . this book broke *all* of the rules. It broke all of my creative processes. It broke my brainstorming process. I didn't create a mind-map of what I was going to write for each chapter—I just sat down and wrote. It broke my outlining process (which was very sparse to begin with). I don't even know where that outline is anymore—probably stuffed in a desk drawer somewhere. It broke my writing processes to a degree I can't even explain. I didn't write in chronological order. I didn't write what "should" come next. Hell, I'm not even worried about whether or not this will all tie together to present to the world, wrapped neatly in a nice little box with a bow.

Perhaps "broke" is the wrong word. Perhaps it simply *transformed* everything I've come to know about writing and the creative process—*my* creative process.

This is my book.

This is my art.

This is my *soul*.

With this particular project, I was constantly inspired. Actively inspired. Soulflowingly *inspired*. Nothing you've read here was forced. Each day of writing these words brought a renewed sense of excitement and wonder. Of hope and possibility. Of therapy and release. It was such a privilege—such a *blessing*—to have a project like this to pour my heart and soul into. And, if I'm being totally honest, I'm not even sure I want to go through and edit these chapters . . .

Because your soul can't be edited.

Your soul can't be forced.

Your soul is your soul.

Just like this book is this book.

If I could define soulflow, it would look a lot like this quote: "Maybe the journey isn't so much about becoming anything. Maybe it's about unbecoming everything that isn't really you so that you can be who you were meant to be—who you've always *truly* been—in the first place."

The journey of unbecoming. What an empowering concept—to unbecome the victim, overachievement, consumption, judgment, rejection, attachment, guilt, resistance. To unbecome everything you aren't.

This is me. This is my unbecoming. This is my *soulflow*.

And I sincerely hope it encourages you to surrender your fears, embrace *your* unbecoming, and receive that long-awaited guidance to finally come to the place you've always been . . .

Home.

# acknowledgements

I'm starting on these acknowledgements in tears, just after writing my closing thoughts. I wasn't lying when I said that this book *is* home for me. How blessed I feel to have been able to capture my most intimate thoughts, memories, and experiences through the written word. How blessed I feel to have shared them with you.

First and foremost, I'd like to thank God, The Universe, The Divine Spirit. For the first time in my life, I feel truly awake. Thank you for showing me the quiet power of surrender, vulnerability, and unbecoming. Without these things, I would not have had the courage to write these words. I am forever humbled. Thank you.

To Anna Vera, for being YOU. There's such comfort in knowing that I can text, call, or (now) drive just a couple of hours any time to raise my vibe, get my soul-sister fix, and get grounded again. You have truly been a best friend in every sense of the word. I am so thankful for our friendship and how it has so effortlessly bloomed!

To Samantha Davidson, for being a fountain of support and one of my closest confidantes! You were the first person I shared this book with and I want to thank you for taking the time to read it (and for helping me with the cover—the purple ombré was indeed the missing piece!) I can't wait to see all that you do with **The Write Path**, with your books, and in life! I'm so very proud of you.

To Ray Griffiths—how blessed I feel to have connected on Twitter all those years ago! You're always there to offer words of encouragement and never fail to bring a smile to my face. Thank you for reading an early draft of this book and for being such a phenomenal human being. I'm so lucky to call you a friend!

To my family—Erin, Mom, Paul, Dad, Rachel, Nana and Papa—thank you for supporting this crazy girl and her crazy-big dreams. You are a constant reminder that my worth is not defined by how much I do or don't do, the mistakes I make, or what others think of me. Thank you for loving me and supporting me unconditionally.

To my furbabies—I know you can't read this, but thank you for letting mama write . . . even when the weather was nice and you wanted to play, even when it was late and you wanted to sleep, even when I would burst into tears after writing a chapter and you had no idea what was going on. Your presence will always be a place of solace. You will always be enough for me.

To my Elevate and Valiance clients—Thank you for believing in my coaching programs . . . and in me! Working with each of you has been one of the biggest blessings of my life. I truly cherish our time together and can't wait to see all the good you do in this world!

To my readers, my *tribe*—Thank you for the encouragement. Thank you for the unwavering support. Thank you for showing up on the days when I didn't feel like showing up for myself. Your kind words never fail to lift me up and remind me what we've built together. All we'll ever need is right here. Thank you. I love you.

# *that smart hustle*
## PODCAST

*available on*

 Podcasts

 Spotify

 STITCHER

 SOUNDCLOUD

FOR FREE RESOURCES, COACHING
PROGRAMS AND COURSES, AND MUCH
MORE, MAKE SURE TO VISIT KRISTEN'S
PERSONAL GROWTH WEBSITE:

**WWW.THATSMARTHUSTLE.COM**

Are you ready to start living your life
*on purpose?*

whole **4** challenge

*#soulflowseries*
WHOLE 4 CHALLENGE WITH KM

Sign up for this free challenge at
www.thatsmarthustle.com/whole4

# about the author

Kristen Martin is the International Amazon Bestselling Indie Author of the YA science fiction trilogy, THE ALPHA DRIVE, the dark fantasy series, SHADOW CROWN, and the self-help book, BE YOUR OWN #GOALS. She is also a Business Success Coach for creative entrepreneurs, the founder of That Smart Hustle and Black Falcon Press, and an avid YouTuber with hundreds of videos offering lifestyle advice for aspiring authors and creatives alike.

## STAY CONNECTED:

www.kristenmartinbooks.com

www.youtube.com/authorkristenmartinbooks

www.facebook.com/authorkristenmartin

Instagram @authorkristenmartin

Twitter @authorkristenm

Made in the USA
Middletown, DE
03 November 2019